L. Preston

MAP REA[illegible] AND INTERPRETATION

New edition
Metric

P. SPEAK, M.A., F.R.G.S.
Head of School of Geography

A. H. C. CARTER, B.Sc.
Principal Lecturer

Cambridgeshire College of Arts and Technology, Cambridge

Longman

Foreword to fully revised metric edition

Since this book was first published in 1964, it has been updated many times with a substantial revision and the inclusion of metric examples in 1970. The time has now come for a fully revised and completely metric edition.

The book has been well received by schools and colleges—not only within the United Kingdom, but, somewhat surprisingly, throughout the English-speaking world. Most of the copies are bought as class sets and used by successive groups of students so that we have been astonished to calculate that upwards of five million geography students have made use of *Map Reading and Interpretation*. In this edition we have changed most of the map extracts, but they remain representative of British landscapes specially selected as appropriate in the preparation of candidates for public examinations set within the United Kingdom. We trust, however, that the reader's interest in maps will extend beyond the examination room and that he will acquire a skill of lasting benefit.

The authors in recent years have been involved primarily in the teaching of undergraduate classes of geography, but have maintained close contact with schools and the geography curriculum as chief examiners and assessors at Ordinary and Advanced Level G.C.E. and in the B.E.C. examinations. Although we have welcomed many changes during the past fifteen years in the geography syllabuses, we remain convinced that a firm foundation in map appreciation is an essential part of a general education as well as a base from which more advanced geographical studies can spring. We believe, too, that many students find real pleasure in maps and that, for them, this is the first awakening of an interest in geography. A disciplined study of map reading and interpretation develops useful practical skills and facilitates a realistic reconstruction of the perceived landscape.

As the Ordnance Survey now publishes its main map series only on metric scales we have included in this edition map extracts on scales of 1:25,000 and 1:50,000; the old, so familiar, one-inch map has now become a historical document. Of the maps originally published in the book three have been retained: the Cotswolds, Fenland and Alloa extracts, but in the equivalent metric series. The Ingleborough area map has also been retained, but at a scale of 1:50,000 rather than 1:25,000. The other six maps are new to this edition. We have also included, for the first time, a geology map which covers exactly the same area as the topographic sheet of the Ingleborough area. It should help in the recognition and interpretation of land forms and perhaps help to develop a latent interest in geology. Simplified geology maps are now set in geography examinations by some examining boards. We have updated and amended the text where necessary and included a new section on the Drainage Basin and Stream Ordering: otherwise the text of Parts One and Two remains substantially the same.

The reader should note that a complete revision of the 1:50,000 map series has not yet been made by the Ordnance Survey. On the First Series the contour values are given to the nearest metre, but remain drawn at the old vertical interval of 50 feet: this makes the numbering of the contours irregular and confusing. Annual inspection of the Ordnance Survey's map catalogue is recommended to check the latest revisions.

P.S.
A.H.C.C.
1979

Acknowledgements
We are pleased to record our grateful thanks to those individuals and institutions who helped us in the full revision of this book. At the Ordnance Survey, A. E. Parke provided information on the revision of map series and on metrication. L. H. Wilson, Chief Planning Officer of Warwick and Leamington District Council made available to us maps and other information on which Figures 42a and 42b are based. Chris Warne, formerly of Cambridgeshire College of Arts and Technology, assisted in the drawing of the new maps and diagrams.

Ordnance Survey map extracts and conventional signs are reproduced by permission of the Controller of Her Majesty's Stationery Office, Crown © reserved.

Figure 37 has been redrawn from several sources but is mainly based, by permission of the Geological Survey, on the one-inch geological map of the Ingleborough area.

Plates 1, 2, 5 and 6 are published by permission of Aerofilms, Plate 3 by the Department of the Environment, Crown © reserved, RAF photo, and Plate 4 by the Scottish Development Department, Ministry of Defence (Air Force) Crown ©.

The cover photograph by Noel Habgood is reproduced by permission of J. Allan Cash.

We must also express our thanks to the staff of our publishers at Longman House, Harlow for detailed editorial and art work, and in particular, to Susan Sampford for patient correspondence, encouragement and help at all stages in producing a published work from the authors' manuscripts and illustrations.

Contents

List of figures

List of plates and maps

PART ONE BASIC PRINCIPLES OF MAP READING
Chapter one Scales and marginal information

Map title

Map reading begins by noting the name or title of the map. This may be the name of the most important settlement on the map, the name of the region covered by the map, e.g. the Cairngorms, or the name of an island if this comes conveniently within the compass of one sheet of the map series. On the map extracts given in examinations and on the flat issues of the 1:10,000 plan and 1:25,000 map no title is usually given. On the folded maps published by official bodies such as the Ordnance Survey the title may be given on the front cover and on the spine.

The title gives the location of the map within the British Isles; the student should, at once, turn to the Atlas and refer the map to the wider setting of its regional geography.

The map usually carries numbers or letters that place it within the general framework of all the maps published in the same series at the same scale. By reference to the index diagram in the margin of the map sheet or to the cover of the folded maps any map can be located in this way and the adjacent sheets determined.

Map scale

Now turn to the scale. Unless the student appreciates fully the meaning of scale it is impossible to read the map correctly. The successful representation of the very varied features of the earth's surface on a map is largely a question of scale. The map reader should be able to distinguish, by examining the scale, those features that are shown true to scale from those that are generalised or shown by symbols. He must cultivate the habit of checking the scale whenever a map is examined and will find that, with a little practice, the estimation of distances and areas on maps of different scale is not at all difficult. When travelling by cycle, car or on foot a map should always be carried and distances checked by comparing the mileage indicated on guide posts and milestones with those measured from the map. In this book there are examples of maps published by the Ordnance Survey on scales of 1:50,000 and 1:25,000, but maps are readily available on very many other scales than these.

Scale

This means ratio, proportion or relationship. Scale is the ratio of the distances and areas shown on the map to the corresponding distances and areas on the earth's surface. Let us examine its significance on a map.

All the Ordnance Survey map extracts are overprinted with the National Grid. On the maps in this book the grid lines are spaced at intervals of 1 kilometre. Consider the size of a grid square on the 1:25,000 map and compare it to a grid square on the 1:50,000 map. Although the square represents the same area of the earth's surface it is one-quarter the size on the 1:50,000 map. This must affect the amount of detail to be shown on the maps and the accuracy to which it can be drawn. On the larger Ordnance Survey scales such as the 1:10,000 and 1:2,500 it is possible to distinguish clearly the size and shape of all buildings; street names can be inserted, gardens depicted, large houses and farms individually named and all the detail of industrial plant, railway sidings and quarries fully shown.

On the 1:25,000 and 1:50,000, however, many of these features can only be shown in a general way. Churches are depicted by symbols, only very large public buildings are named, and the detail of railways and mines may be omitted altogether. On these smaller scales such natural features as rivers are generalised and almost all man-made features shown by symbols. On the 1:50,000 map a line 0.5 millimetre thick represents a distance of 25 metres so that the map width of the symbol often greatly exceeds the width of the feature on the ground. Measure the widths of railways, roads, rivers (near the mouth and at intervals upstream), buildings, etc. on 1:50,000 and 1:25,000 maps and work out from the scale the actual distances in metres represented by these measurements.

On the 1:50,000 map, First and Second Series, Ministry of Transport roads over 4 metres wide are shown by a symbol giving a ground representation of 50 metres. Very few roads come anywhere near this width. On the 1:25,000 map the ground measurement of the Motorway symbol is about 30 metres and so these wide highways may be shown to scale.

Scale may be shown on maps in three ways:

(I) *By a representative fraction, or R.F.*

This is usually shown as a ratio, e.g. 1:50,000, or alternatively as a fraction, $\frac{1}{50,000}$. The numerator of the fraction is always one unit and the denominator is the number of the same units on the ground represented by one unit on the map.

The R.F. is perhaps the best way of showing scale since it avoids mention of any unit of measurement and should prevent any confusion in converting metric scales to imperial units, and vice versa. Before the Ordnance Survey decided to adopt the metric system for almost all its maps and plans it was often necessary to construct scale-lines to show kilometres and metres for use with the imperial scales. Reference to the R.F. made this possible, and for the convenience of all map users the new Ordnance Survey metric maps show alternative scale-lines reading to a scale of miles—see Fig. 1. The necessary calculation for the 1:50,000 scale is as follows:

Scale of 1:50,000 means that one unit on the map represents 50,000 units on the ground.

One centimetre on the map represents 50,000 centimetres on the ground and 2 centimetres on the map represents 50,000 × 2 = 100,000 centimetres, i.e. 1 kilometre.

A scale-line to read to 1.7 kilometres must therefore be drawn to a length of 3.4 centimetres.

Now to construct a scale line to read to 1.7 miles at a scale of 1:50,000:

50,000 inches on the ground is represented by one inch on the map.

There are 63,360 inches in a mile and so:

1.7 miles, or 107,712 inches on the ground is represented by $\frac{107,712}{50,000} = 2.1542$ inches.

A line drawn to this length can then be divided to show mile, half-mile and tenth-mile units as in Fig. 1.

Note that a scale of 1:25,000 is *twice* that of 1:50,000 and allows more detail to be shown. The rule is: the higher the denominator of the R.F. the smaller the scale so that for a map of given size the 1:50,000 scale will show four times the area covered by the 1:25,000.

(II) *By a scale-line*

This is usually a plain scale of convenient length suitably marked into primary divisions with one division only marked into secondary divisions. This forms a backward-reading unit to the left of the zero mark, and complete subdivision of the forward-reading units is therefore avoided. The use of the scale-line is clearly demonstrated in Fig. 1.

On the full sheets published by the Ordnance Survey a scale-line is provided in the lower margin of the 1:10,000 and 1:25,000 series and in the side margin of the 1:50,000.

(III) *By a statement*

two centimetres to one kilometre; one inch to one mile; half-inch to one mile.

The use of the statement to indicate scale is declining with the introduction of the decimal system. The Ordnance Survey now publishes only tourist maps at the one-inch scale and only one map sheet (the Snowdonia National Park) at half an inch to the mile.

Metric scales

No single scale of map can serve the needs of all map users. The Ordnance Survey produces a wide range of scales, each one serving primarily a different purpose, and the practice of continual revision has been introduced in order to keep the map information as up to date as possible. The Survey has a responsibility for

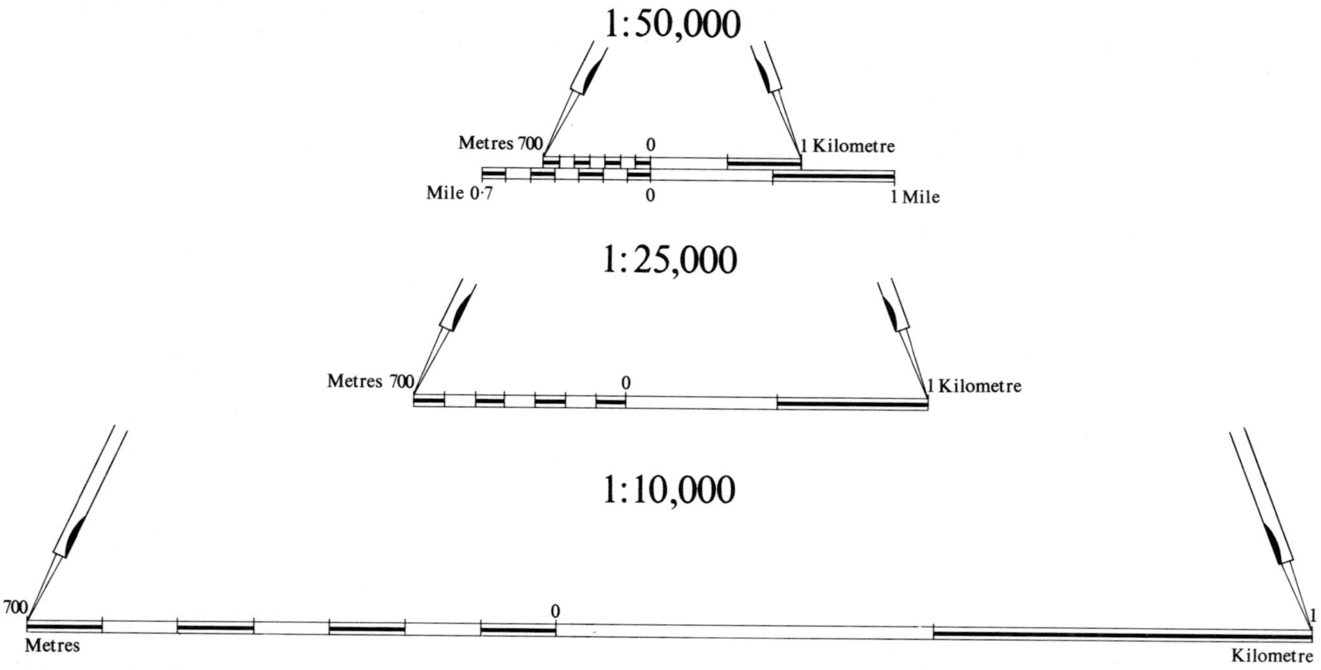

Fig. 1 Metric scales. The dividers are set to measure 1.7 kilometres.

surveying and publishing maps of Great Britain: it is a Government agency, founded in 1791 to make maps for military and scientific purposes. Its principal publications at the present time are as follows:

Small-scale maps

1:1,250,000—An outline map of Great Britain.
1:1,000,000—The one to a million international series map covering Great Britain in two sheets.
1:625,000 —Great Britain administrative areas and route-planning maps.
1:250,000 —Nine sheets covering the whole country and designed mainly for the motorist.
1:100,000 —Outline administrative county maps.
1:63,360 —Maps of special areas for tourism and recreation.
1:50,000 —A national series for the general map user.
1:25,000 —A complete series with excellent topographical detail, ideal for the walker and for field study and regional planning.

Large-scale maps and plans

1:10,000 —The largest scale covering the whole of Great Britain used for civil engineering, in local government and for town and country planning.
1:2,500 —A series covering all Great Britain except mountains and moorlands. All man-made features of the landscape shown true to scale.
1:1,250 —The largest scale in any series covering all towns and urban areas with a population of about 20,000 and over. Any feature covering more than 8 square metres is shown in plan.

Measurement of distances

A pair of dividers should always be used to take straight-line measurements off the map. Pieces of cotton, string or wool may stretch and give a reading far from accurate. Compasses are also unsuitable since the pencil point may itself represent some 30 metres on the scale. Should the subdivision along the scale be inadequate for the accuracy of the measurement required, or should the scale-line be missing, then the R.F. must be used to convert the map measurement to ground measurement in the following manner:

What is the distance 'as the crow flies' from Aston Somerville church, grid reference 048379 to the church at Snowshill, grid reference 097337 on the map of the Cotswolds (Map 4), scale 1:50,000?

Distance taken from the map = 10.9 centimetres
Ground distance represented = $10.9 \times \frac{50,000}{100,000} = 5.45$ kilometres
(N.B. 100,000 centimetres = 1 kilometre)

Remember that on O.S. maps the normal grid lines are 1 kilometre apart. Straight-line distances east–west and north–south on these maps can be given very quickly in kilometres by counting the lines across the map or by consulting the grid numbers in the margins of the map. On the 1:25,000 and 1:10,000 maps the marginal lines of the map are diced at 100-metre intervals thus permitting measurement to one-tenth of a kilometre.

Measurement along roads, railways and rivers

Distances along a winding road or river must be broken down into a series of short straight-line measurements, from bend to bend. A piece of strong cotton or thread could be used but the straight edge of a piece of stout paper is to be preferred.

Start with one corner of the paper, and at the end of each straight section, pivot the paper on a pencil point and rotate to the next straight section. This method avoids inaccuracies due to the free movement of the paper. See Fig. 2.

When the measurements are complete apply the paper to the scale-line and read off the total distance.

For short measurements this method is quite satisfactory, but over longer distances errors are likely to occur as there will be bends in the roads and the rivers that the map-maker was unable to show because of the limitations of scale. This is particularly true on scales smaller than 1:10,000.

Railway distances generally involve less difficulty since most railways follow more direct routes involving fewer bends and no sharp changes in direction.

A handy inexpensive map-measurer—the opisometer, can be obtained from most bookshops and stationers. This consists of a small wheel with counting dial calibrated in metres and kilometres. A pointer ticks up the distance as the measure is wheeled over the map.

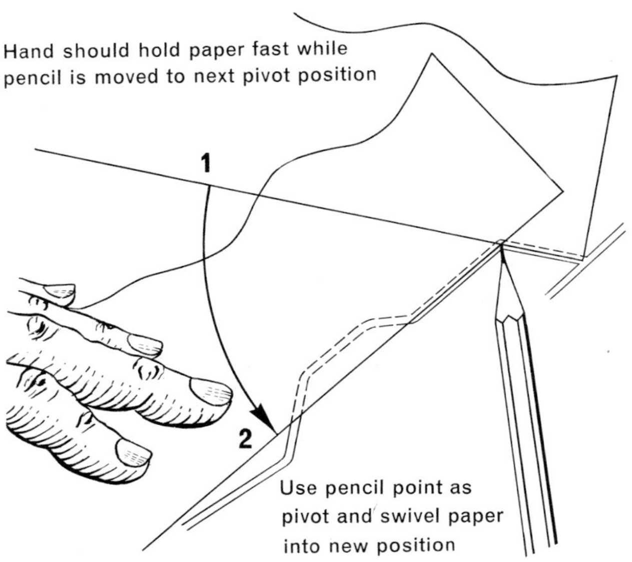

Fig. 2 Method of measurement along a winding course.

Always check the setting of the dial by first running over the scale-line. If there is a discrepancy between the number on the dial and the values given on the scale-line, then after taking your measurements from the map run back the pointer to zero along the scale-line, noting from the scale-line the distance travelled. With cheaper models this may be necessary in any case since the counting dial may not be present.

Conventional signs

The limitations of scale on a map should now be clear. Whenever it is impossible to show clearly, and to scale, any feature that is an important landmark, then the map-maker must choose a symbol or conventional sign to represent it. Many of these are familiar to all map-users: churches, railway-lines, roads, sand-pits and quarries, windmills, etc.

The regular map-user learns to recognise these signs by continual reference to map and landscape. The student is strongly recommended to check the map information in his home area and to prepare in his notebook lists of symbols and their meaning. The symbols can be divided into two major groups:

(i) landscape features—e.g. symbols portraying communications, drainage, vegetation, buildings, mineral workings, etc.;

(ii) non-landscape features—e.g. boundary lines, latitude and longitude, methods of showing height, etc.

Characteristic sheets of the symbols used on O.S., 1:25,000 and 1:50,000 maps are given on pages 66 and 67.

National Grid

All post-war maps published by the Ordnance Survey are overprinted with a grid of kilometre squares that forms an excellent reference system to any place in the British Isles. The whole country is covered by primary squares of 100-kilometre side and these are subdivided into 1-kilometre secondary squares. For any place in the British Isles the same grid line intersection will appear on all the relevant maps published on different scales, so that no matter which map is used the grid reference will always be the same. The diagram Fig. 3a explaining the origin of the National Grid should be studied carefully. A similar diagram, explaining the method of using the National Grid is given in the lower margin of all O.S. maps and this note is usually printed with the map extracts used for examination purposes.

The grid numbers start from a point to the west of the Scilly Isles, and the position of any place can be given in terms of its distance east and north of this origin. The numbers running west to east along the top and bottom of the sheet are called eastings: those running from south to north along the right and left margins are called northings. When giving any reference always take first the eastings numbers and then the northings. Thus to refer to a kilometre square a four-figure reference can be given made up of the easting and northing bounding the square to the left and bottom—e.g. 5806 for the square containing Point A in Fig. 3b. This is the Normal Kilometre Reference.

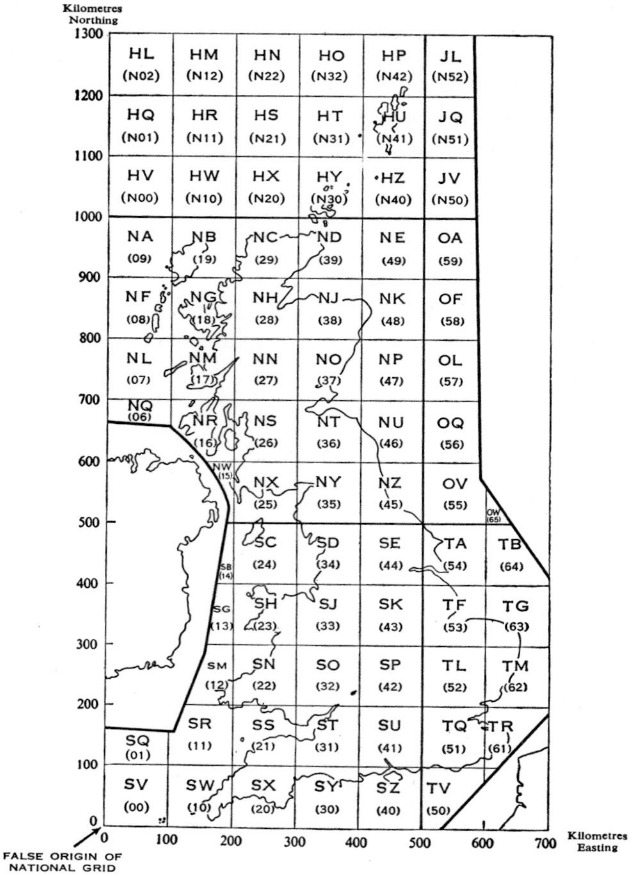

Fig. 3a The National Grid and Reference System.

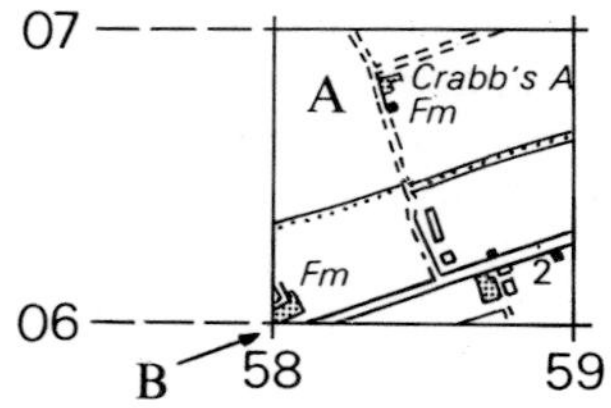

Fig. 3b How to give a grid reference.

For more precise location to within 100 metres a six-figure reference is needed. This is called the Normal National Grid Reference and is obtained by estimating the 'tenth' subdivisions of each square on the 1:50,000 map, but on the 1:10,000 and 1:25,000 maps a marginal strip is subdivided into these 100-metre intervals. Both references would be repeated in each 100-kilometre square so that in order to make each reference unique the grid letters must also be given. These are shown in Fig. 3a and always prefix the normal reference to produce the Full Kilometre and Full National Grid References. They will apply to one square and one point only in the British Isles.

On map extracts and around the margin of the map sheets the letters may be missing and it is then necessary to use the small figures printed in the map corners. (These numbers appear in the appropriate squares below the letter in Fig. 3a.)

Points A and B in Fig. 3b are taken from the 1:50,000 Fenland sheet (Map 3) and can be used to demonstrate the different ways of giving a map reference.

Point A. Normal National Grid Reference 583068
Point A. Full National Grid Reference TF/583068
or 53/583068
Point B. Normal National Grid Reference 580060
Point B. Full National Grid Reference TF/580060
or 53/580060

The Full Kilometre Reference to the grid square on the map is TF/5806.

Direction

Direction is studied best with the map and compass in the field. The student should take a 1:50,000 map of his home district and climb the nearest summit. This may be a church tower or the top of a high building in flat country. The map must be set by identifying at least three prominent features in the landscape with the corresponding features on the map. Taking the top of the map as north one can obtain the general direction of the compass. If a hand compass is available it is possible to set the map more accurately. If the legend in the lower margin of the map-sheet is consulted the angular differences between Grid North, True North and Magnetic North, in the four corners of the map can be found. The compass points to Magnetic North so that the map must be moved round until the compass needle coincides with Magnetic North on the map. Allowance must be made for the annual variation of Magnetic North from True North at the point of observation.

Figure 4 shows a typical direction indicator found in the lower margin of Ordnance Survey maps. The differences between Magnetic North, Grid North, and True North may be stated as follows:

Magnetic North —the direction in which a compass needle points.

ORIENTATION

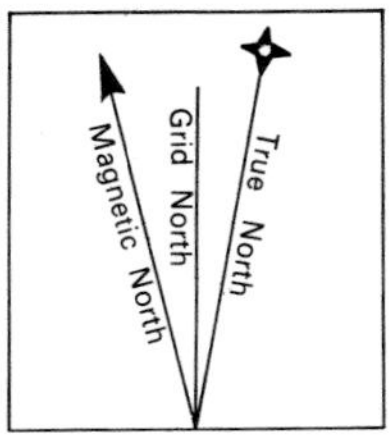

e.g. 1:25 000 Second Series, Tenby extract

True North

True North is 2° 09′E of Grid North

Magnetic North

This was about 7°W of Grid North in 1976 decreasing by about ½° in four years.

Fig. 4 True North, Grid North, Magnetic North.

Grid North —the direction of the grid lines on the map.

True North —the direction of the north pole.

At the present time the Magnetic North Pole lies to the west of the True North Pole as seen from the British Isles and the difference between the poles is best expressed in degrees. This difference is the magnetic variation and it will, of course, vary from place to place on the earth's surface, even within the area shown on a 1:50,000 map, so that the value given for it usually indicates the variation at the centre of the map. A further complication arises because the magnetic variation changes also with time and so the annual variation of the compass at any point must also be known. This is why the procedure outlined above must be followed if a correct compass bearing or accurate setting of the map is to be achieved.

Direction can also be found on all Ordnance Survey maps by examining the meridians of longitude and the parallels of latitude. On the whole sheets the map border shows the values of latitude and longitude and with a ruler it is possible to join up the corresponding points across the map to produce a network of meridian and parallels called a map graticule. Map extracts, however, do not contain these points and such a construction is not really necessary in any case as the map contains, here and there, a small lightly drawn cross which marks the intersection of the lines of latitude and longitude at that point. An example of such an intersection can be seen at grid reference 114335 on Map 4. The upright line points True North and is part of a meridian which intersects the True North Pole, and the horizontal line runs truly east to west. Note that the grid lines do not, at any point correspond with these graticule lines so that they give only a very general indication of direction.

For indicating direction in examination answers it is generally satisfactory to use the points of the compass. Measurement in degrees is not usually required. Figure 5a shows sixteen points of the compass with the corresponding angular bearings. Note that bearings are given as part of the 360° of the full circle, reckoned clockwise from Magnetic North. There should be no confusion over giving a bearing if one remembers that direction is given *from* one place *to* another—e.g. in Fig. 5b.

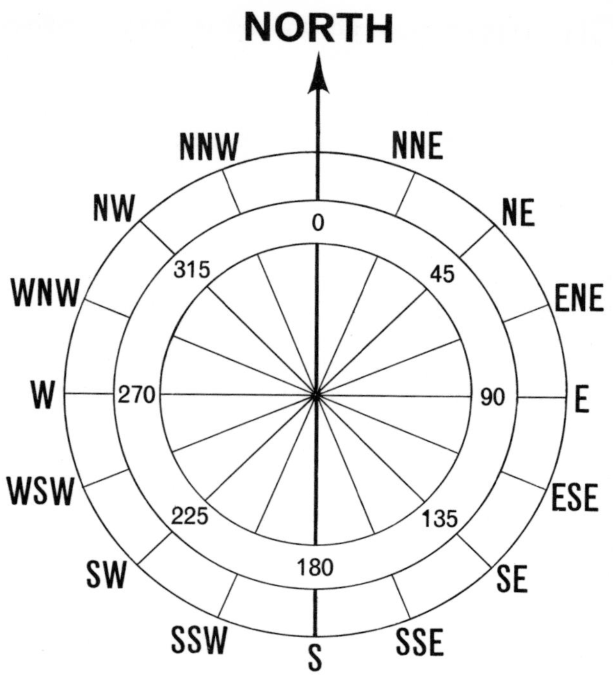

Fig. 5a Compass points.

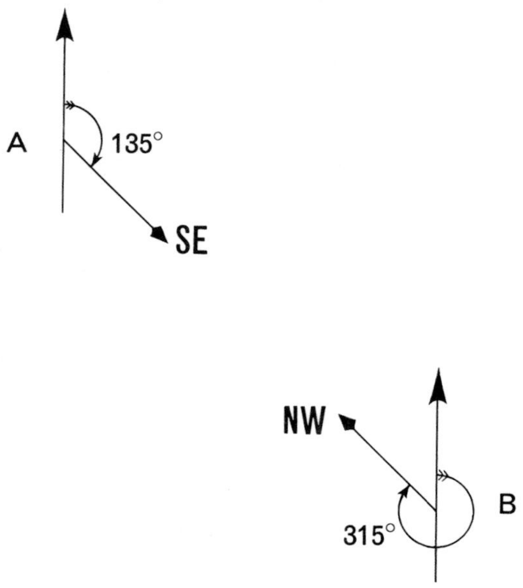

Fig. 5b Direction on the map. Direction from B to A is north-west, and direction of B from A is south-east. But direction between A and B must be north-west-south-east.

Chapter two Map measurement

Measurement of areas

If we wish to calculate the area of land or of sea, or perhaps of a lake, or the extent of woodland shown on the map, simple graphic methods can be employed.

The squares method

Transfer to tracing paper an outline of the area to be measured and cover with small squares, all the same size. In the example, Fig. 6 below, taken from Map 7 of the Cairngorms, quarter kilometre squares have been drawn. On this tracing of the 1:50,000 map each square will represent 0.25 square kilometre. Place a tick in each complete square as indicated. Those squares that are broken by the map outline can be dealt with by a 'give-and-take' method—e.g. in Fig. 6 count square A as a complete square and cancel square B. The land has been 'taken' from B and 'given' to A to make the whole square. Account for all the other 'broken' squares in the same way, count the number of ticks and convert to square measure. For an approximate answer in square kilometres this method could be applied directly to the map by counting the grid squares.

The strip method

Use strips of equal width instead of squares as in the previous example. The 'give-and-take' principle is applied in the same way to both ends of each strip but it is easier to apply, because the 'broken' areas are so much smaller. To obtain the total area, add together the lengths of all the strips and multiply by the width of one strip. See Fig. 7.

The success of both these methods depends on the care taken in tracing the map outline and the skill in applying the 'give-and-take' method.

Map copying and reduction

Every student should be able to copy a map and to reduce it to a given fraction of its original scale. He can then transfer selected detail from the published map to his own sketch map, keeping an overall accuracy of scale. Examination questions frequently ask the candidate to reduce a map to half-scale and to insert the principal relief and drainage features or some detail of the human geography.

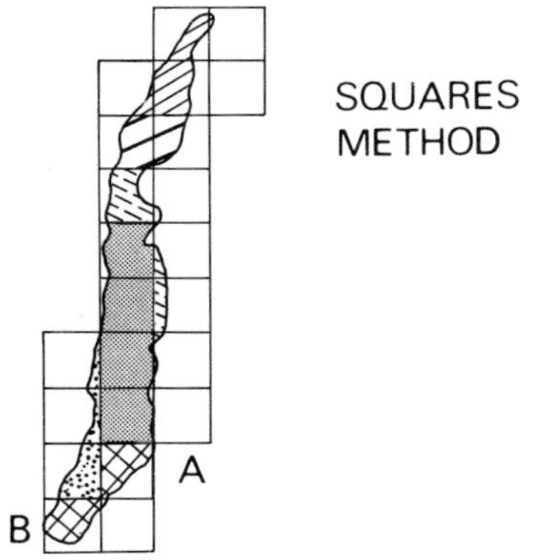

The shading indicates the complementary squares

Approximate area of Loch Avon = 0.56 km^2
(9 squares 0.25 km × 0.25 km = 0.5625 km^2)

Fig. 6 Measurement of areas: by squares method.

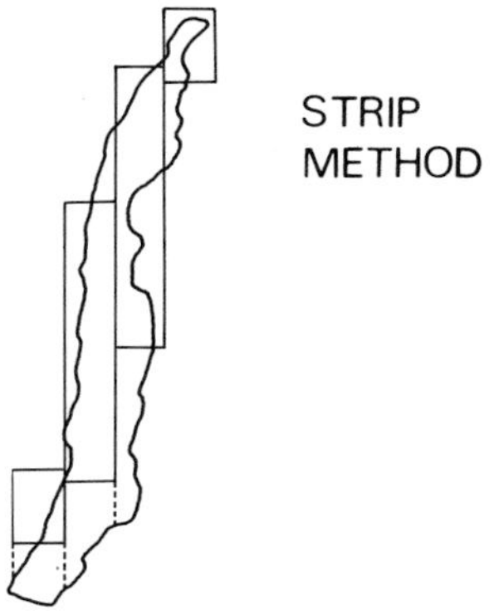

The total length of all strips is 58 mm and the width of each strip is 4 mm (20 mm = 1 km)

Approximate area of Loch Avon = 0.58 km^2
(58/20 km × 0.20 = 0.58 km^2)

Fig. 7 Measurement of areas: by strip method.

As such great care has been taken over scale in plotting the original map any sketch map used in map analysis is obviously better drawn to scale than roughed out freehand. With a little practice, copying and reduction can be done quickly and accurately. All the map figures in this book have been drawn to scale and this is indicated either by the representative fraction or by a statement below each one. Figures 31 and 38 are examples of half-scale reductions.

Copying

The copying of a map is best done on tracing paper but this method may be forbidden in the examination room. An alternative method makes use of the kilometre grid covering the map by marking off the grid line intervals along the edge of a piece of paper. Measure the external dimensions of the sheet and rule and number the grid lines. Select the features to be shown, note where they cross the grid lines on the map and draw in the corresponding position on the sketch.

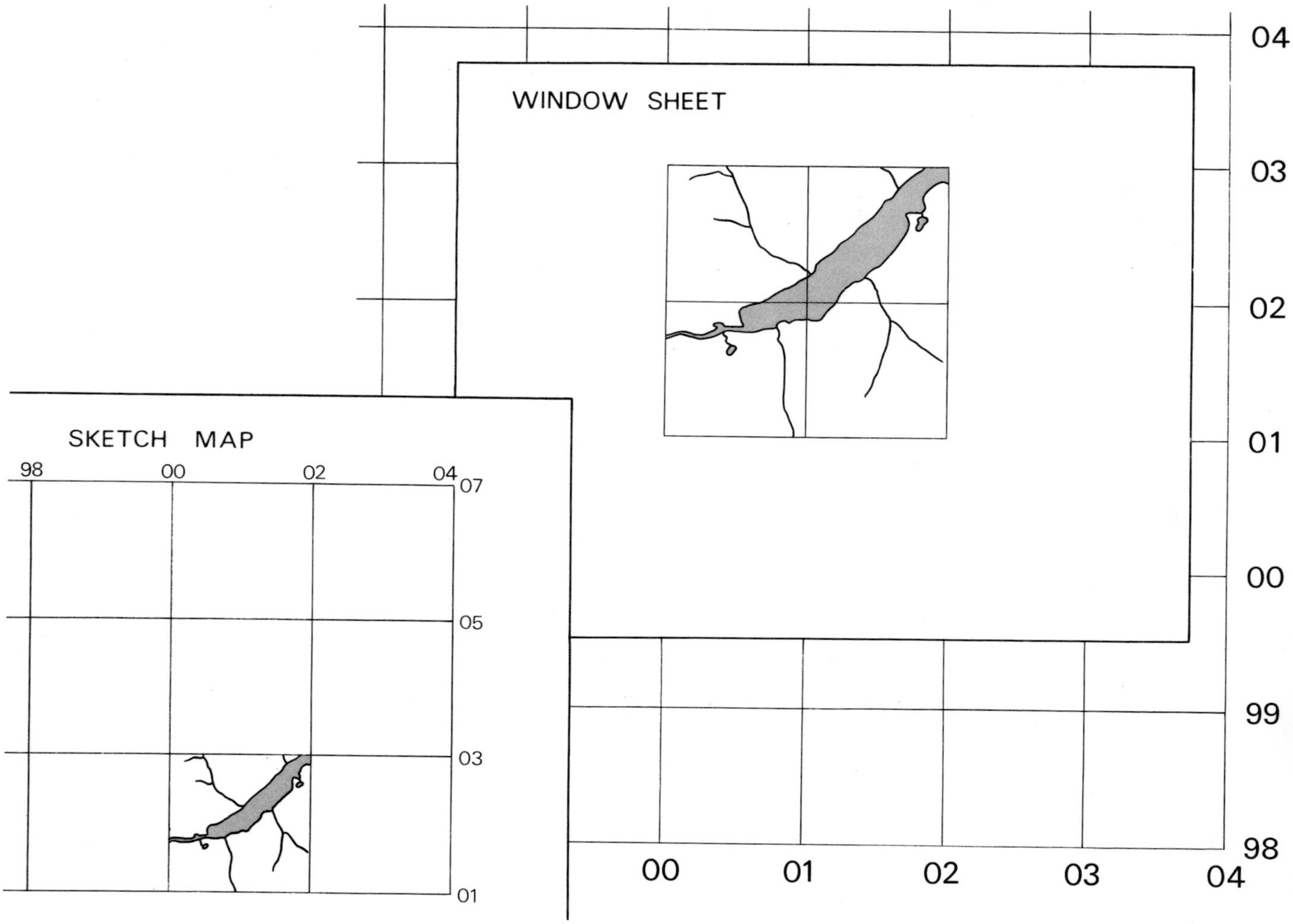

Fig. 8 Reduction of a 1:50,000 map to half-scale.

Reduction of a map to half-scale

This can be carried out in a similar way. Figure 38 is a reduction to half-scale of the 1:50,000 map of the Ingleborough map (Map 6), to show the main drainage features. Note that only the alternate grid lines appear on the reduced map so that four squares on the original are represented by one square on the sketch. It will be seen that the distance between the lines on the reduction is the same as between the grid lines on the map but they are numbered differently. Notice, however, that often the margins of the map extract are not grid lines but lines falling somewhere between. These odd strips should be dealt with first, measuring their width with a ruler, halving them and transferring them to the sketch. If the number of squares along the margins of the map extract is also odd, the odd ones, too, should also be halved and transferred. On the 1:50,000 reduction when adding detail concentrate on four of the map squares at a time, covering the rest with sheets of loose paper. In a class, or at home, a sheet of paper with a 'window' square cut from the middle is very useful in transferring features from map extract to sketch. An example of the method is given in Fig. 8, for a scale reduction of the 1:50,000 map.

To cut the 'window' simply fold your paper across the middle and lay it on the map, ticking the width of two grid squares near the centre of the paper. Cut down each tick to the length of one square and cut across. Unfold the paper to reveal a window the exact size of four of the map squares.

Reduction of the 1:25,000 map to half-scale

After the difficulties of the 1:50,000 reduction the 1:25,000 presents little trouble. The grid squares on the map are large enough to be individually reduced. As in the case of the 1:50,000 the main map extract should be reduced first, any odd marginal strips dealt with next and the full squares last. No actual measurement is necessary, however, for any process, the margins of the 1:25,000 map carrying divisions in grid 'tenths'. If these are counted and subdivided very accurate lengths can then be set off with a pair of dividers without the use of a ruler except for the drawing of straight lines. *Note* that grid numbering on the 1:25,000 sketch will be the same as on the extract and detail will be transferred to the reduction square by square. Figure 31 of the Pershore 1:25,000 map has been reduced to half-scale and this reduction should be consulted.

Enlargement of the map may be carried out in the same way but satisfactory results are not possible because of the scale difficulties. We have seen already that on small scales much detail is generalised or shown by symbols. It is clearly impossible to make an accurate enlargement of such features.

No sketch map, enlargement or reduction is complete without a title, north arrow, and simple short scale-line to indicate the new scale, or this may be given as the new representative fraction.

Chapter three Representation of relief

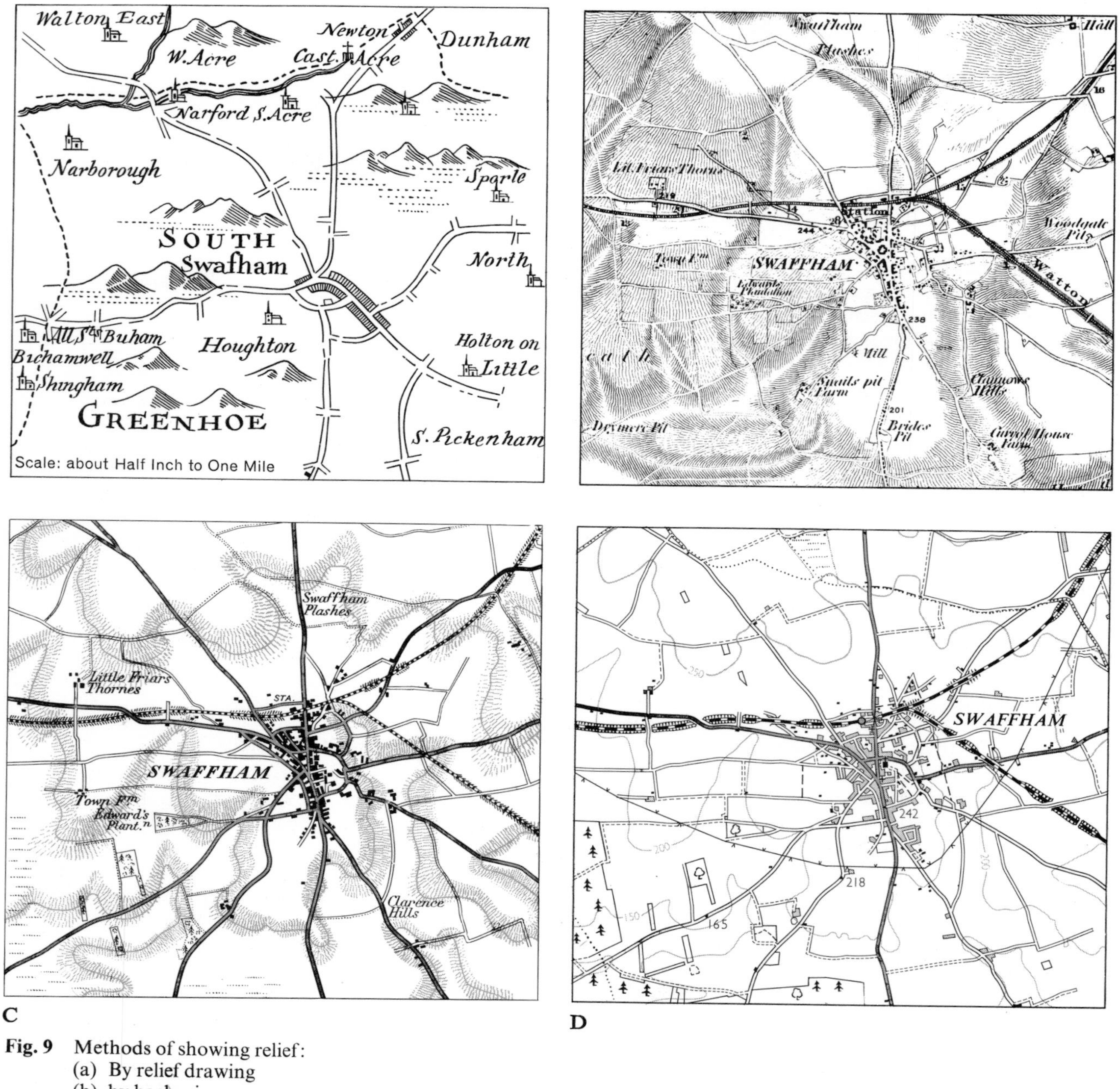

C

D

Fig. 9 Methods of showing relief:
(a) By relief drawing
(b) by hachuring
(c) by hill shading
(d) by contouring.

Relief is the shape of the ground surface and a good method of relief portrayal must show not only the height of the land but also its shape and gradient, so that individual land forms can easily be recognised. The best method for topographical maps is undoubtedly the contour which combines height and slope. Earlier methods were chiefly pictorial and inaccurate. Until accurate surveying instruments were invented no other methods were possible.

One of the earliest techniques was Relief Drawing where hills were drawn in profile and lightly shaded to suggest height and bulk. Other shading methods assume a light shining obliquely on the landscape so that some slopes are in shadow and others unshaded are in the light. Yet another technique is by hachures—lines drawn on the map in the direction of the steepest slope and the steeper the slope the closer are the hachures drawn.

These methods of representing relief all suffer from the loss of accuracy in the detail required by modern maps unless supported by another technique such as the contour line. Moreover, the density of the shading on drawings is often such that it obscures other detail and makes overprinting of names extremely difficult. Comparisons of these techniques with the contour can be seen in Figures 9a, b, c and d.

In this book the maps show relief by contours, trigonometrical points, bench marks and spot heights. In the special Tourist Editions published by the Ordnance Survey selected contours are chosen to mark the divisions between coloured layers, the colours ranging light to dark from low to high ground. This system of layer-colouring is used to great effect in the small-scale maps of most atlases. On some of the Tourist Maps the layer-colouring is supplemented by oblique hill-shading, assuming the source of light near the ground in the north-west.

A map has two dimensions only; the third dimension, height must be shown pictorially so that the form of the land can be read at a glance by the experienced map user. The only true representation of relief would be on a plaster or plastic model.

Contours

A contour may be defined as a line on a map joining all points the same height above Ordnance Survey Datum Level. For the present map issues published by the Ordnance Survey ordnance datum is the mean sea-level recorded at Newlyn in Cornwall. The interval between successive contours should remain constant on any one map sheet, and on all maps published in one edition. On O.S. maps the contour interval is 10 metres on the 1:50,000 map and 5 metres on the 1:25,000 and 1:10,000. This is known as the Vertical Interval or V.I. To assist the map reader, contour lines are thickened at regular intervals; every 50 metres on the 1:50,000 map and every 25 metres on the 1:25,000. Any confusion arising out of contour reading should readily be removed if it is remembered that to walk along a contour would be to follow a level path, and by leaving the contour one must rise or fall.

The geographer is closely concerned with slopes and land forms. Where contour lines are close together the slopes are steep, and conversely where the lines are distantly spaced the slopes are gentle. If the contour lines are spaced at regular intervals the slope is even. The closer the contour lines the more the slope angle approaches 90 degrees. If the slope is vertical the contour lines will merge, e.g. in sea-cliffs and quarry faces. Slope patterns produced by actual ground surfaces are shown in Fig. 10.

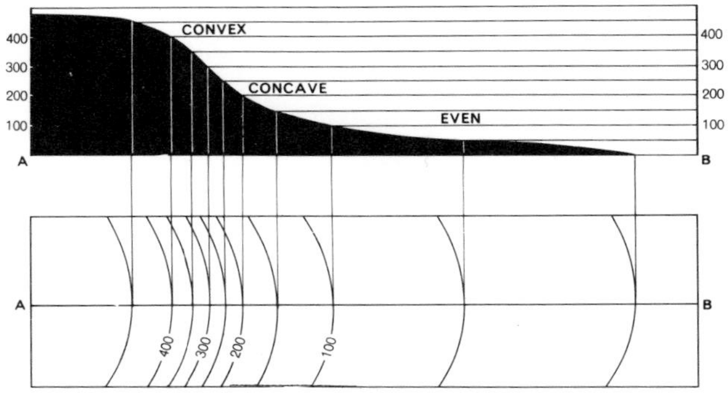

Fig. 10 Slope patterns.

The limitation of the contour is seen on the Fenland map (Map 3) with its V.I. of about 15 metres. On this sheet most of the land is below 15 metres with only two contours appearing on the edge of map and the relative differences of height (so important in a low-lying area) are then shown by selected spot heights.

Trigonometrical stations, bench marks and spot-heights

These are points accurately surveyed and shown as heights above mean sea-level by points on the map, with the actual height in metres appearing on the map by the side of all spot heights and selected trigonometrical stations.

Trigonometrical points or stations

Distances are surveyed by angular measurements and the ground distance calculated by trigonometry. The surveyors erect concrete pillars on the summits of the hills which act as the corners of the main triangles of the Survey. Church towers and other high buildings are also used. These are the trigonometrical stations seen on the maps and they can be used for revision of detail at any time.

Bench marks

These may be found cut in 'benches' usually walls, gate-posts or the sides of buildings. The height of each bench-mark above sea-level has been accurately determined by a levelling process to within 1/100th of a foot, though the decimal places are not given on the small-scale and medium-scale maps included in this book.

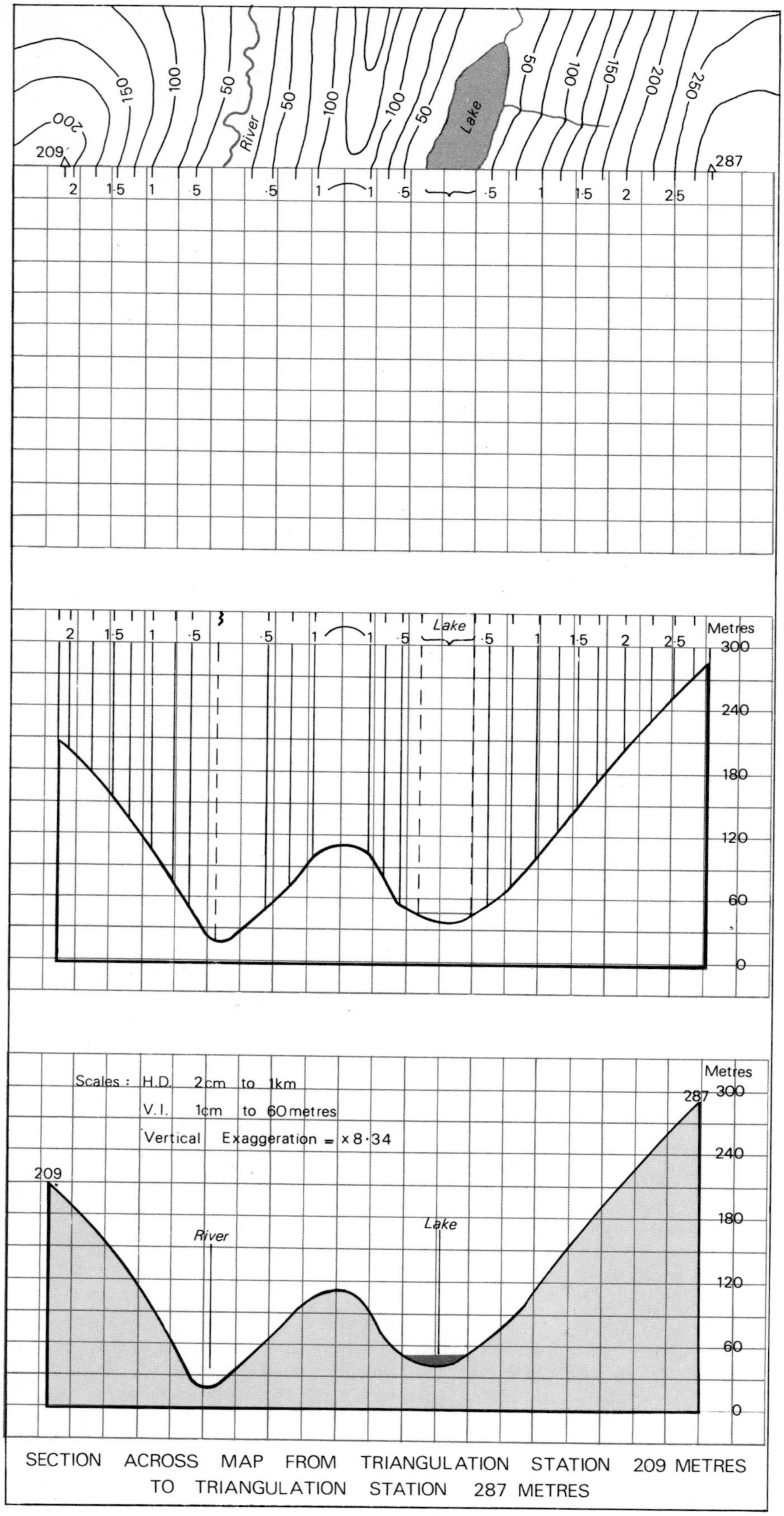

Fig. 11 Construction of a cross-section

a Rule in pencil a line linking the two ends of the section. Place the edge of the graph paper along the line of section so as to position neatly your profile in relation to the sheet as a whole. Tick off the crossing points of contours and label with the correct height. Also carefully mark the position and extent of other features, e.g. rivers, lakes, etc.

b Draw a base line equal to length of section by dropping guiding verticals from the end ticks. Choose a suitable vertical scale and raise the ends of the section at least 10 metres above the highest contour, cut by the line of the section. Drop vertical guide lines from each tick along the margin to correct height on section profile. Join up the lower ends of the lines to produce a smooth final profile.

c Tidy up the section profiles by rubbing out all guide lines. Label clearly important features. Attach title, details of scales; colour land and water features.

Spot-heights

There is no physical evidence of spot-heights in the field but they appear frequently on maps, along roads and between contours and near sea-level to aid interpretation between the contour interval and are shown thus—.431.

Section drawing

A cross-section

The shape of the land surface is brought out very well by the construction of a vertical section along a line drawn on the map. Significant breaks of slope may be revealed on the section that otherwise would be hidden from the map observer. The section may be annotated to indicate important features of drainage or land-use. An example of a cross-section taken from the map of Ingleborough (Map 6) is given in Fig. 13.

Method

Take the edge of a piece of graph paper and mark carefully where the contours cross the line of section. Number the contours as shown in Fig. 11a. Erect a vertical scale to your section-block, choosihg an interval that does not give too great a vertical exaggeration. For the 1:50,000 map a scale of 10 millimetres to represent 100 metres is quite suitable. In upland regions there is really no need for the vertical scale to start at sea-level. Keep the horizontal scale the same as that of the map. Drop vertical lines as shown in Fig. 11b (with experience lines on the graph paper can be used) to the heights along the section and join up by a smooth line. Shade the section to give the impression of solidity, and finally give a title to the section and indicate the scales used. See Fig. 11c.

The vertical exaggeration on a section can be calculated as follows:

The R.F. of the map is 1:50,000

$\therefore$ 1 millimetre on the map represents $\frac{50,000}{1,000} = 50$ metres

Let 10 millimetres represent 100 metres on the vertical scale.

Then vertical exaggeration $= \frac{500}{100} = \times 5$.

A sketch-section

Measure the length of the section and construct a section block. The line of section may be drawn in by eye estimating the rise and fall of land, from careful inspection of the contours. Such a profile can be drawn in an examination where there is no time to carry out the detailed procedure of the cross-section. Although no fixed vertical scale is used, some indication of height along the profile is desirable. An example of this kind of section taken off the map of Fort William (Map 8) is given in Fig. 12. Always fix the section by quoting grid references at both ends.

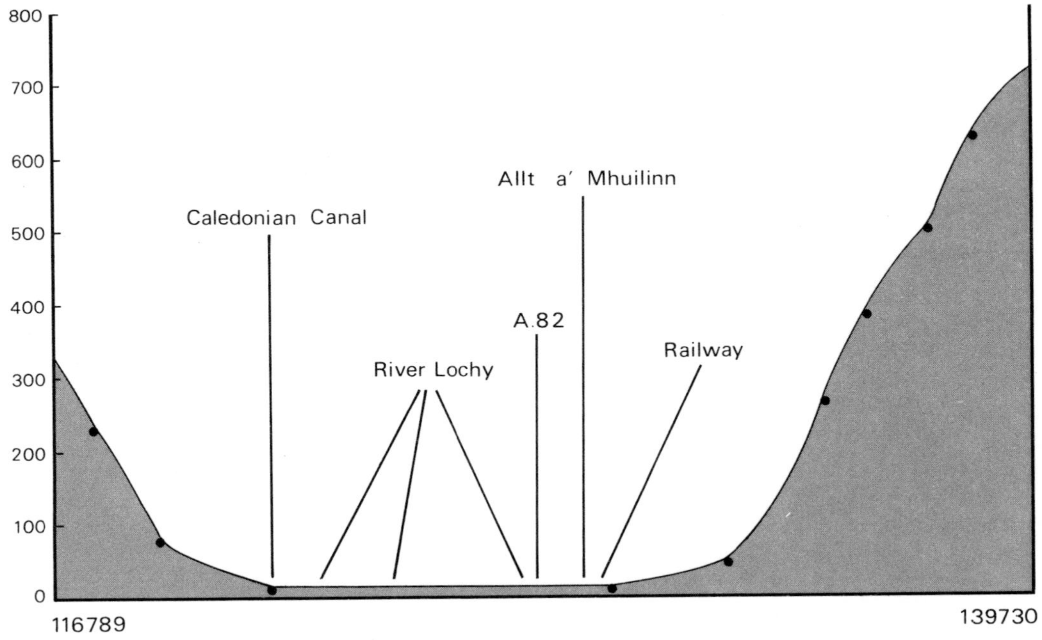

Fig. 12 Sketch-section across Fort William map from Meall Bhanabhie 116789 to Meall an t-Suidhe 139730.
Countours plotted at marked breaks of slope.
Vertical scale 1 mm to 10 metres.

Intervisibility

Section drawing can be used effectively to discover whether two points are intervisible and to reveal 'dead ground'. A series of sections can be made to show the total area visible to an observer from one hill top. In Fig. 14 drawn from the map of Ingleborough (Map 6) the observer on West Fell G.R. 721784 would see clearly to the summit of Ingleborough Hill, G.R. 741746, but much of the low ground in the valley of the river Doe, would be hidden from view and constitute 'dead ground'.

Gradients

The degree of slope or gradient of sketches of roads, rivers, hill and valley-sides can be measured directly from the map. Gradient is expressed as a proportion, the vertical distance in terms of the forward distance: e.g. 1 in 10; 1 in 20; 1 in 30, etc. A vertical face would have a gradient of 1 in 0 and a horizontal surface of 0 in 1. The vertical and horizontal units must always be the same so that on O.S. maps the horizontal units must be converted to metres. To obtain the gradient along a road or hill-side, measure the forward distance between the top and bottom of the slope and convert to metres. Then calculate the difference in height between the two points from the contour values and by simple division the gradient is determined. An example is worked out overleaf. Note that on the 1:50,000 and 1:25,000 maps a single arrow is placed across roads with gradients 1 in 7 to under 1 in 5, and a double arrow where the gradient is 1 in 5 or steeper.

It must be pointed out, however, that the method described above contains an inherent error since the forward distance measured is not the slope distance but the horizontal equivalent. The error is negligible except in truly mountainous country—e.g. for a slope of 1:15 the error on the map is only 0.2 per cent.

The horizontal equivalent

All slope measurements taken by surveyors in the field are reduced to the horizontal equivalent and ultimately to sea-level. It is as though all the distances were taken along a plane at sea-level. The meaning of horizontal equivalent can be seen from the diagram, Fig. 15.

The distance shown on the map will be AB and not AC, the surveyed and actual distance. In regions of subdued relief the differences will be slight and can be ignored; but in mountainous country keep the horizontal equivalent always in mind when climbing. If you set out to walk to the top of Cairngorm (005040) from White Lady Shieling (995053) on the map of the Cairngorms (Map 7) and allow for the reduced speed of ascent, you will underestimate your time of arrival unless you remember that the measured distance is short of the actual distance to be covered.

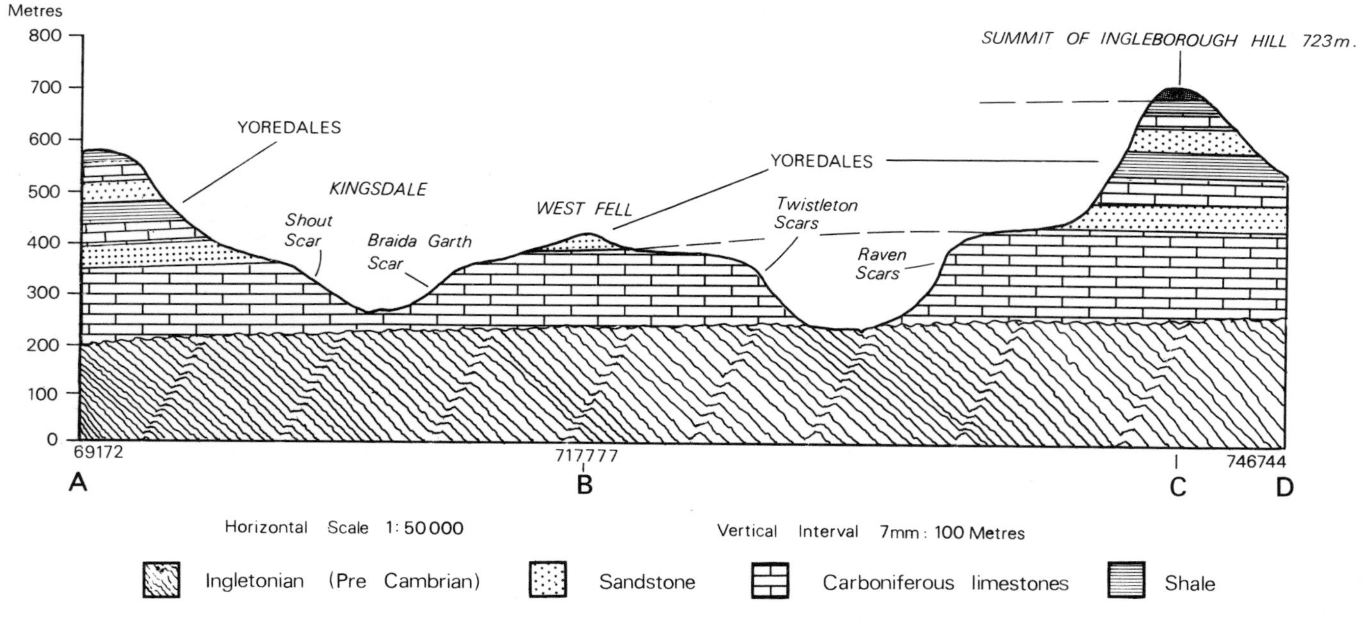

Fig. 13 Cross-section to show the geological structure of Ingleborough.

Calculation of gradient from Map 8

Calculate the gradient of the footpath from the Club House (137762) to the Mountain Rescue Post (167723):

Distance by footpath, i.e. horizontal distance—4.9 kilometres

= 4,900 metres

Difference in height, i.e. vertical distance

= 650 metres

Average gradient $= \frac{4,900}{650}$

= 1:7.5 approx.
or 13 per cent

This is a very moderate gradient and presents no difficulty to the mountain walker, but note that it is the average gradient and some parts of the route are steeper than this.

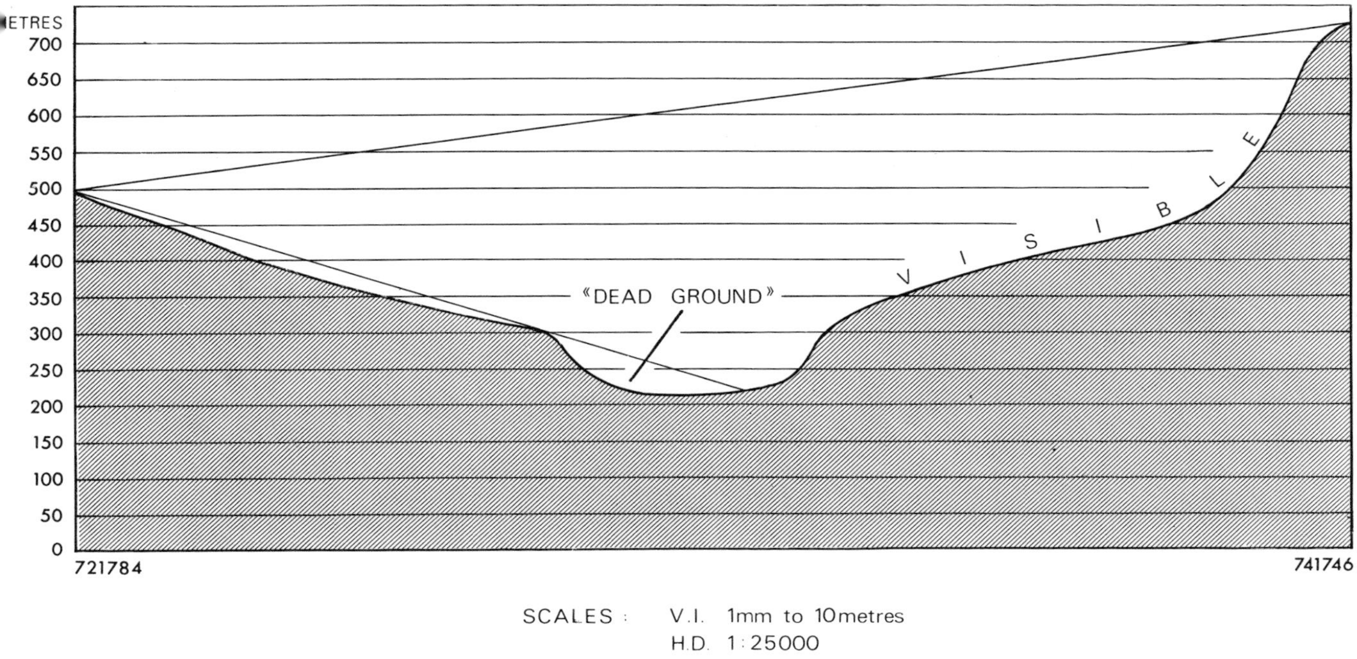

Fig. 14 Intervisibility and 'dead ground'.

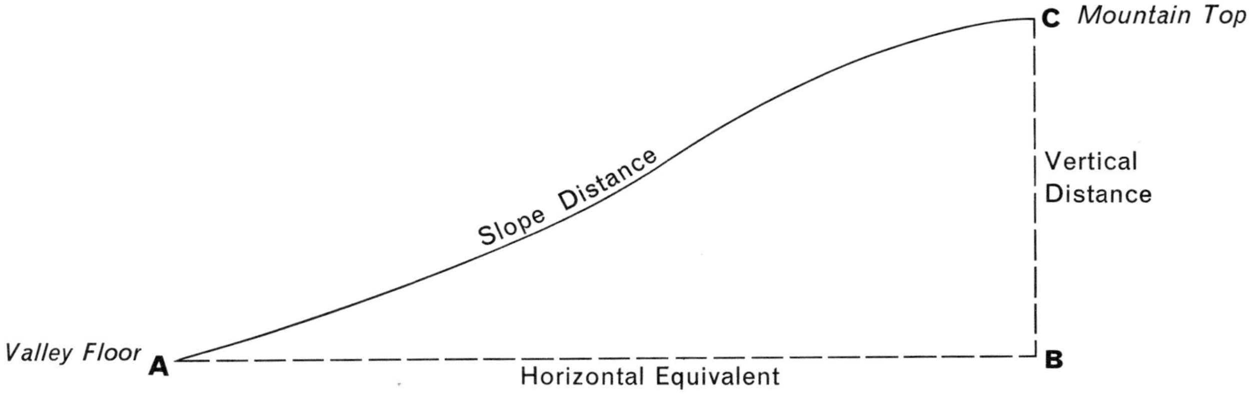

Fig. 15 The horizontal equivalent.

Questions on Part One

1. Metric measure:
   How many millimetres in a metre?
   How many centimetres in a metre?
   How many metres in a kilometre?
2. Construct a scale-line to read to the nearest 100 metres for a 1:10,000 map.
3. What distances on the ground are represented by the following measurements taken from a 1:50,000 map?
   1. 9.2 centimetres
   2. 4.4 centimetres
   3. 1.6 centimetres

   and from a 1:25,000 map?
   4. 10.6 centimetres
   5. 4.6 centimetres
   6. 2.7 centimetres.
4. Measure the distances by road on the Fenland map (Map 3) between the parish churches of Downham Market (613033) and Outwell (513037).
5. Measure the distance by rail on the Fenland map (Map 3) between Downham Market Station and the mineral line junction.
6. Measure the distance along the coast on the Tenby map (Map 2) from Giltar Point (125983) to Bowman's Point (137016) at the limit of mean high water.
7. State the direction in degrees and by the points of the compass of the following features from the summit of Ben Macdui on the Cairngorm sheet (Map 7): Rothiemurchus Lodge (952069); White Lady Shieling (994053); Hutchinson Memorial Hut (023998); The Angel's Peak (953977); Falls of Dee (945991).
8. List all the O.S. symbols and their meanings appearing in grid squares 1300 on the Tenby sheet (Map 2) and 9192 on the Alloa sheet (Map 9).
9. Calculate, in hectares, the area of land shown on the map of Tenby (Map 2). N.B. 1 square kilometre = 100 hectares.
10. Reduce to half-scale the map areas limited by grid lines as follows: (a) on the Fenland map (Map 3)—eastings 56 to 61 and northings 02 to 06; (b) on the Cotswolds map (Map 4)—eastings 00 to 04 and northings 33 to 37. Insert all details shown by symbols and give reduced scale-line and new R.F.
11. Reduce to one-third the scale, the map area limited by grid lines as follows: on the Pershore map (Map 1)—eastings 93 to 96 and northings 42 to 45. Insert the river Avon, one contour and Birlingham village.
12. Consult the Cairngorm map (Map 7) and list the various ways in which height and relief are shown. What is the maximum range of relief shown on the map?
13. What additional ways of showing relief could be used with advantage on the Fort William map (Map 8)?
14. Keeping the horizontal scale the same as on the map and using a vertical interval of 2 millimetres to 10 metres construct on graph paper cross-sections along:
    (i) grid line easting 87 on the Alloa map (Map 9);
    (ii) grid line easting 83 on the North Downs map (Map 5).

    Indicate important features crossed by the line of section.
15. Draw a sketch-section along grid line northing 35 on the Cotswold map (Map 4), marking the river, railway and main road.
16. Determine whether you could see Dumbleton church (017357) from the church at Snowshill (096337) on the Cotswold map (Map 4).
17. Draw a sketch-map using Map 4 to show how much of the small hill at Dumbleton is visible from Broadway church (095373). (At least two intervisibility sections will be necessary.)
18. Calculate the average gradient of the footpath from Crina Bottom (723735) to the summit of Ingleborough Hill on Map 6.
19. Assume that you can walk along a flat road at 6 kilometres per hour. Give a reasoned explanation of the time it would take you to walk from Thornton in Lonsdale (686725) along the Kingsdale road to the northern edge of the Ingleborough map (Map 6).
20. To what destination would the Post Office send letters addressed simply by the following grid references? All necessary maps are in this book; the first two figures are references to the 100-kilometre squares and appear in the margins of the map extracts.
    1 The Rector —42/068343
    2 The Warden —17/127718
    3 The Manager —17/121749
    4 The Coxswain —22/138006
    5 The Secretary —53/618013
    6 The Laird —26/935979
    7 The Head Teacher—51/840549
    8 The Matron —42/285658
21. Calculate, to the nearest 0.25 square kilometre, the water area of Lochs Linnhe and Eil on the Fort William map (Map 8).
22. What compass bearing should an aircraft fly along if the pilot wished to follow a grid line from south to north across the Tenby map (Map 2). See Fig. 4, page 9.

PART TWO MAP INTERPRETATION
Chapter four Recognition of land forms

The extent to which the student can pass from map-reading to the correct map interpretation of land forms is dependent on his knowledge of physical geography. In all examinations in Geography for the General Certificate of Education, questions are set on this branch of the subject and the candidate should be acquainted with the more important processes of land sculpture that mould the face of the earth. In this chapter only the briefest mention of these processes can be given. The requirements of the syllabus at Ordinary Level are covered in *Physical Geography*—P. Speak and A. H. C. Carter. Sketch Map Geography: Longman, 1980, and students are referred to this work.

The surface features of the earth are the product of two sets of forces, those acting within the earth's crust and those acting at the surface. Forces acting within the crust are responsible for the general shape or outline of the major land forms, but in Britain and in many other landscapes, the external forces of rivers, ice, wind and the waves of the sea are more significant in moulding the present-day features. At the present time in Britain the principal agents of erosion are fast-flowing rivers and the waves continually breaking on our shores, but a map of any Highland region will give some indication of the work of ice in the form of valley glaciers that were present during the last Ice Age, and even in lowland areas there is often a thick mantle of glacial deposits obscuring the form of the underlying rocks.

In describing the physical features of the map, use must always be made of the special technical vocabulary learned in the lessons on physical geography. Avoid a general description in loose colloquial style. The more common features to be seen on Ordnance Survey maps are listed below with definitions adapted from *Glossary of Geographical Terms*, compiled by a Committee of the British Association, edited by L. Dudley Stamp, Longman, 1961 (3rd edn 1979).

Definitions of common land forms

Col: A marked depression in a line of mountains or hills.

Drainage-Basin: The area drained by a river and its tributaries.

Escarpment: A land form with sides sloping in opposite directions consisting of a steep scarp slope and a more gentle dip or back slope. Highest part is called the crest. The term cuesta is now widely used to describe the same feature. (Cotswolds Map 4 and Fig. 18a)

Floodplain: A plain bordering a river formed of deposits of sediments carried down by a river.

Hill: An elevation generally under 600 metres.

Knoll: A small hill, more or less rounded in form.

Mountain: A natural elevation—of the earth's surface rising more or less abruptly—generally over 600 metres in Britain. It may terminate in a marked summit.

Pass: Col or saddle providing a route-way through a line of hills. It may be at a high or low level.

Plateau: An elevated tract of comparatively flat or level land. When cut up by streams it is a 'dissected plateau'.

Ridge: A long and narrow stretch of elevated ground.

Saddle: A similar depression to the col but generally higher, broader and sloping more gently from the summit.

Spur: A projection of land from high to low ground.

Valley: A long depression between stretches of high ground usually occupied by a stream. If streamless it is a 'dry valley'.

Watershed or water-parting: The line separating the headwaters of rivers flowing in different directions. It may or may not coincide with the crest-line of the relief. See Fig. 18b.

On the map we must learn to recognise the characteristic land forms by interpreting the contour patterns and the other methods used of showing relief. In the remainder of this chapter block diagrams accompanied by contour sketches illustrate the most common British land forms and all references to them are given in bold type.

The landscape of river erosion
Slopes, valleys and spurs

The most common and the most easily identified land forms are **valleys** and **spurs**. Figures 16a and 16b show the shape taken by the contours of typical examples of these features. A valley is immediately recognised if it is occupied by a river, but a dry valley may be mistaken by the inexperienced map-reader for a spur, as the contour patterns are the same. Any difficulty is removed by consulting the contour values and it will be seen that in the valley the contours bend back up-valley in the shape of a 'V'; in the spur the 'V' is towards lower ground. The recognition of slopes as **convex, concave** and **even** has been discussed in Chapter 3, Fig. 10. These are shown along a spur in Fig. 16b, concave along the lower slope, an even section in the middle and convex on the upper slope; this form is frequently found in nature. Make a list of the many excellent examples to be found on the Hollingbourne map (Map 5).

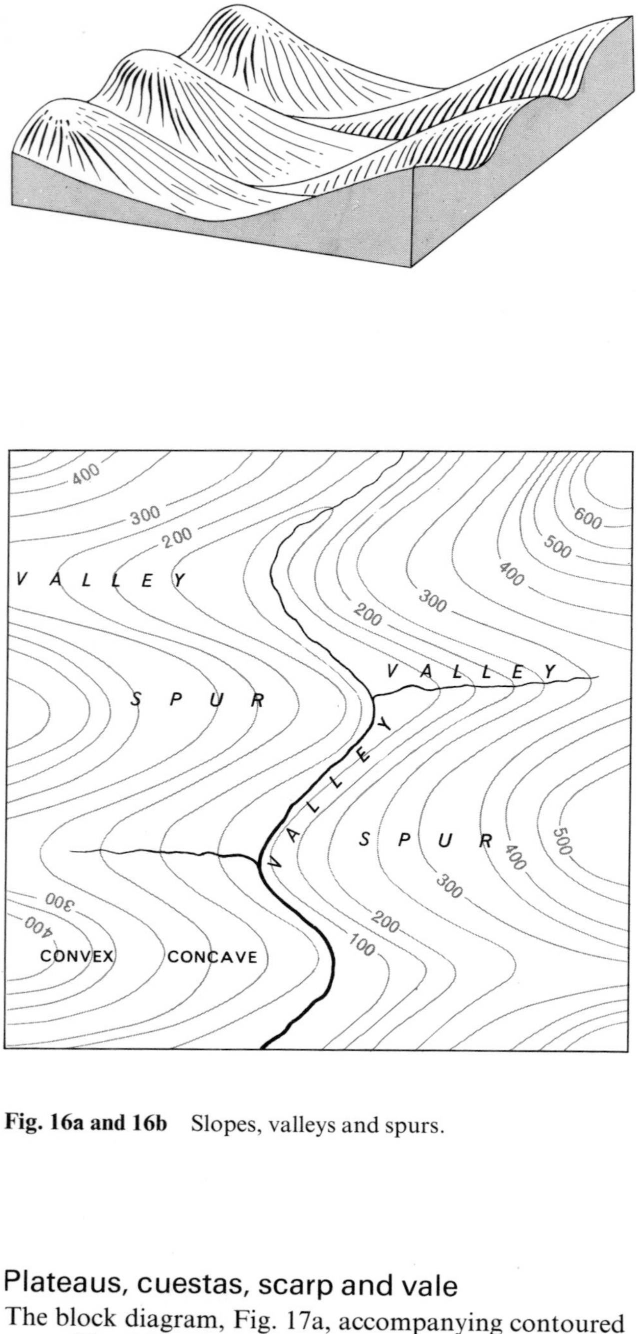

Fig. 16a and 16b Slopes, valleys and spurs.

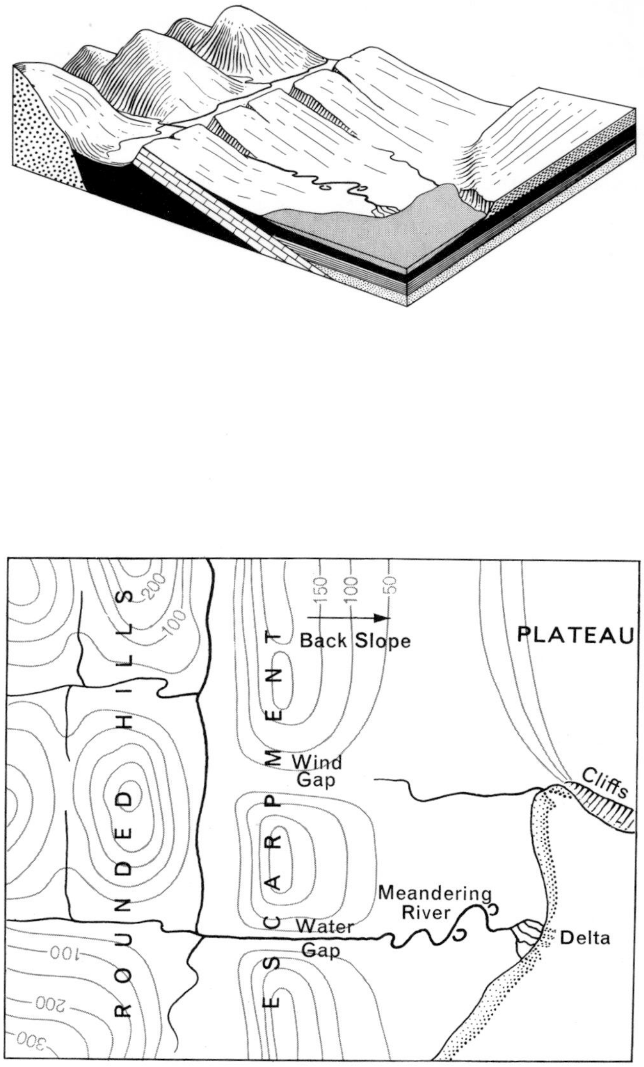

Fig. 17a and 17b A landscape of river erosion.

Plateaus, cuestas, scarp and vale

The block diagram, Fig. 17a, accompanying contoured map, Fig. 17b, show these related land forms. They occur in regions of unfolded rocks that have been raised above sea-level and are undergoing erosion. The rocks are usually sedimentary (e.g. limestone, sandstone, shale), though lava plateaus are also known, as in the plateau of Antrim, Northern Ireland. Where the rock strata lies more or less horizontal the land may appear as a flat-topped plateau. Where the rocks are gently inclined the weaker rocks will be removed by weathering and river erosion more rapidly than the resistant ones which frequently stand out boldly in a **scarp face**, rising to the **crest** of the **escarpment** and falling more gently down the **dip** or **back slope**. The true dip slope is the angle which the actual rock strata makes with the horizontal and few true dip slopes are found in the landscape. The term back slope is to be preferred. The differences between the true dip slope and the more common back slope are illustrated in Fig. 18a. The combined land form of the scarp and back slope is known as a **cuesta** or **escarpment**. The lowland, often wide and extensive, at the foot of the scarp, is called a **vale** and many examples can be seen in Britain, e.g. The Vale of Evesham beyond the **scarp edge** on the map of the Cotswolds. (Map 4.)

Water and wind gaps

These are often of considerable importance as they provide route-ways through ranges of hills. **Water gaps** are seen at once by the roads and railways using them, running alongside the river. **Wind gaps** are similar features, once occupied by rivers but now abandoned except perhaps for a minor stream or patch of marshland. See Figures 17a, 17b and 18a.

Cols, passes and saddles

All three are found in mountain regions and may owe their origin to ice action subsequently smoothed in outline by weathering and stream erosion, but frequently result from the cutting back of streams on either side of the watershed. They may be the only means of access from one valley to another and are used by trackways, roads and occasionally by railways. Good examples can be found on the Cairngorms map. (Map 7.)

River valleys

Ordnance Survey maps are most valuable in showing the varied features of river erosion and deposition. According to features which are present we can recognise the stage of development reached by the river and its valley.

Youthful valleys

Fast-moving streams erode rapidly the rocks they cross, creating deep, steep-sided **V-shaped valleys**, and are said to be **youthful**. The long profile of such streams will show irregularities where harder bands of rock outcrop, and waterfalls or rapids may result. See Maps 7–8 and Fig. 19.

Mature valleys

Mature rivers erode laterally and their valley cross-section is more open, the summits rounded and the valley floor wider than in youth. The river will swing from side to side, undercutting **river cliffs** on the outside and building up mudbanks and water meadows on the inside of its bends. See Fig. 19.

Old-age valleys

The **senile river** has great volume, carrying seawards a heavy load of rock particles. Only a little erosion is now carried on and there is much deposition along the banks of the river and across the broad **flood plain**. **Ox-bow lakes** indicate old river courses and the valley floor, contained in low, smoothed hills is wider than the belt of present meandering. In Fig. 19, the main characteristics are shown, but it should be noted that not all rivers exhibit the three stages of development. Some, like many mountain streams, are entirely youthful whereas others, such as the Trent and the rivers emptying into the Wash, have no youthful stage at all. See Map 3, Fenland.

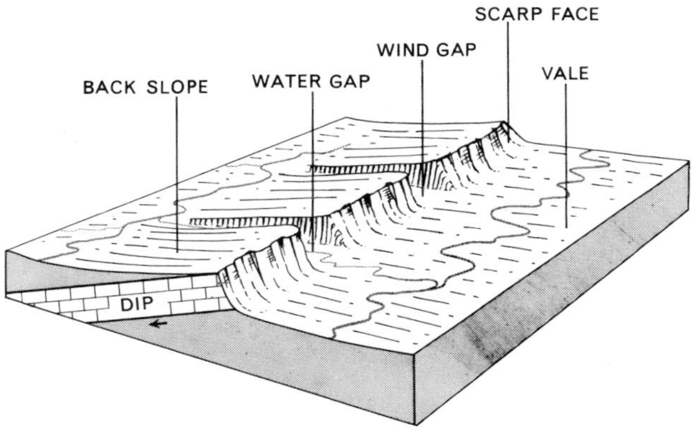

Fig. 18a Scarp and vale. The diagram illustrates the relationship between true rock dip and the back slope of the escarpment.

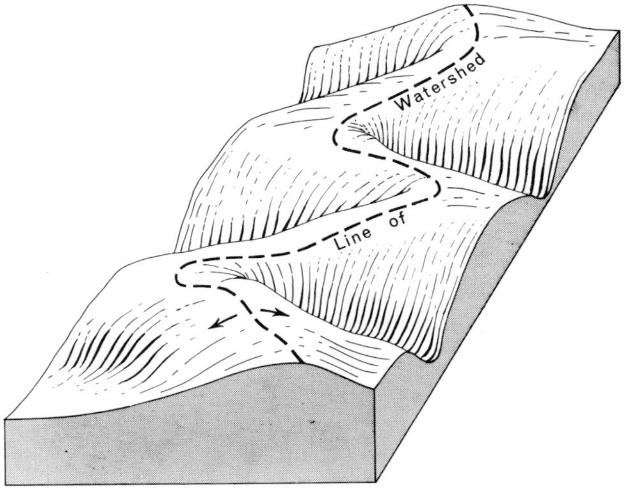

Fig. 18b The watershed. Streams cutting back into the upland have produced a zig-zag line.

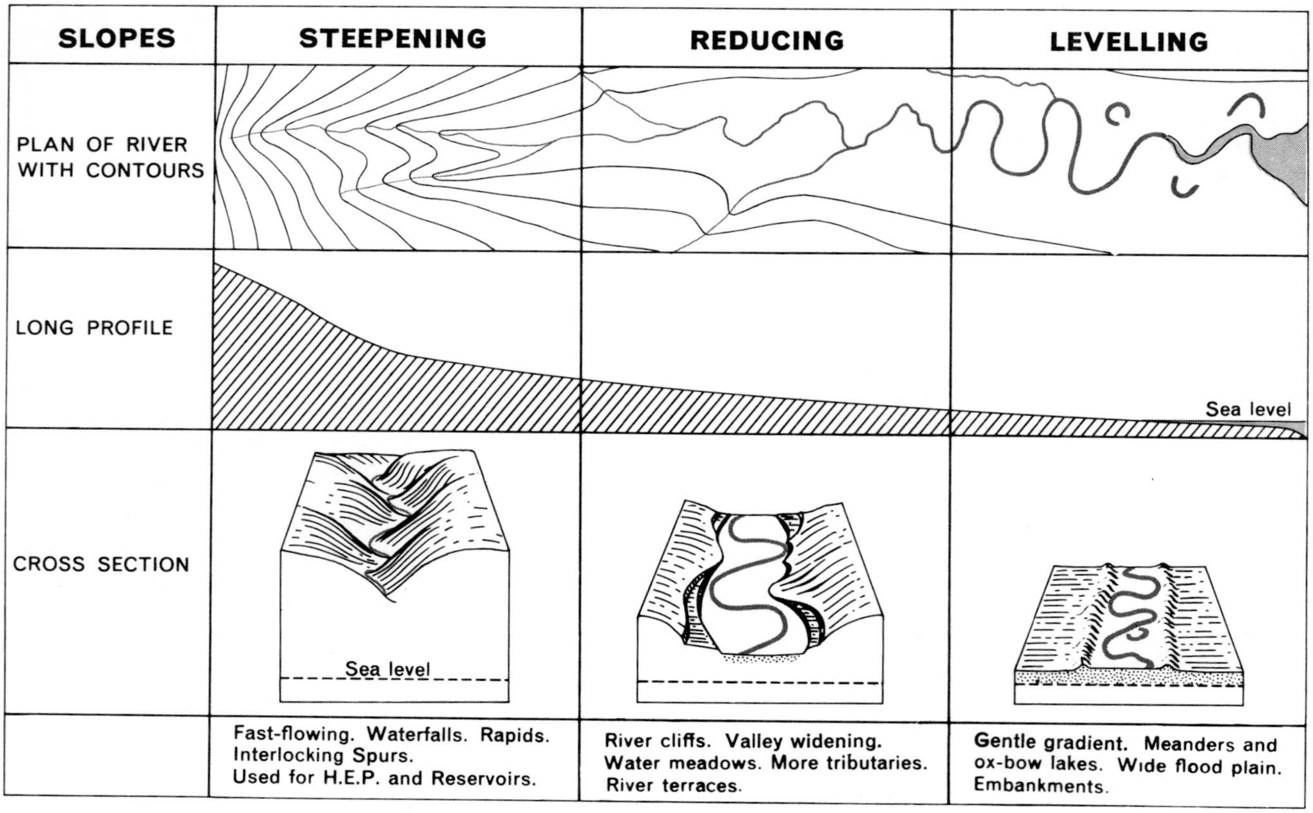

Fig. 19 Characteristics of rivers and their valleys.

The drainage basin

That area of the earth's surface drained by a river and its tributaries is called the drainage basin. It includes not only the present stream channels but also the land between the streams (the interfluvial areas) where ground-water moves through the soil and rock into the streams themselves. The drainage basin is defined by the watershed (see Fig. 18b) and is frequently pear-shaped; it may be drawn for a complete river system where the base level is sea-level, or for a tributary system where the base level is the junction with the main river, or for a river system draining into a lake. Great care should be taken in the drawing of the watershed from a map: the general rule is to space it midway between stream courses draining to adjacent river systems. But if high rock outcrops occur near the course of a river it makes good sense to allow the watershed to follow the outcrop of rock. It is also permissible to draw a 'drainage' basin network for an area where the valley system is today completely dry, for example in the chalklands shown on the Hollingbourne North Downs map (Map 5). These valleys were cut by running water in past times and the pattern of tributary and main valleys resembles closely those of wet valley systems. But in other areas of dry valleys such as the massive Carboniferous Limestone (page 28 and Ingleborough map), where the drainage and valley system is discontinuous and streams disappear below ground through swallow-holes, the drawing of a drainage net is much more difficult and unreliable.

In 1945 an American engineer Robert E. Horton demonstrated a number of ways of measuring the characteristics of the drainage basin, and these have been widely adopted since that time to aid map study of landscapes of river erosion. The method of stream numbering shown in Fig. 20a is one adapted from Horton's studies by Arthur N. Strahler, professor of geography at the University of Columbia, New York.

In this system each finger-tip tributary is designated 1, a first-order stream, and when two first-order streams meet they form a second-order stream. When streams of second order meet they become third order—and so on. The numbers, therefore, increase progressively downstream, but it should be noted that a single stream of a lower order does not change the number of the stream it flows into. It may be surprising to learn that, in the United Kingdom, there are very few drainage basins with rivers greater than fifth order.

With this technique it is possible to describe the shape of the drainage basin in simple mathematical terms and so to express more precisely than can mere description,

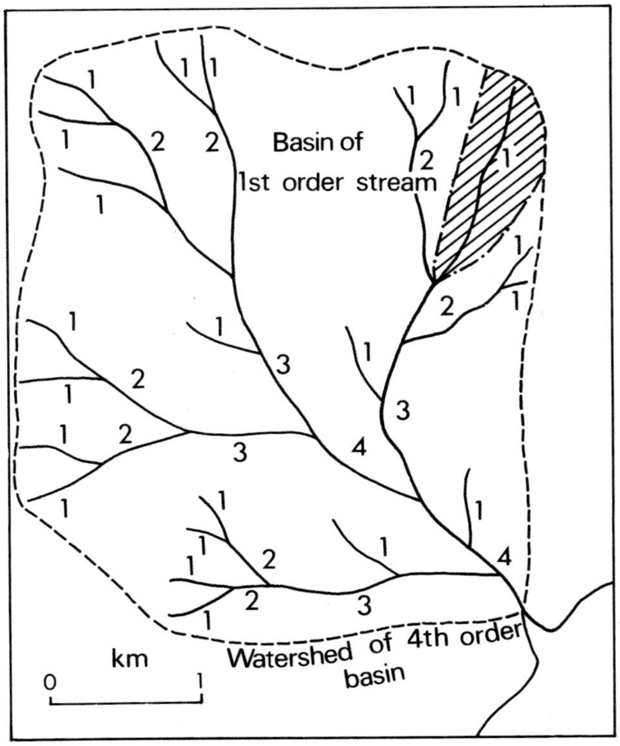

Fig. 20a Stream numbering in a fourth-order drainage basin.

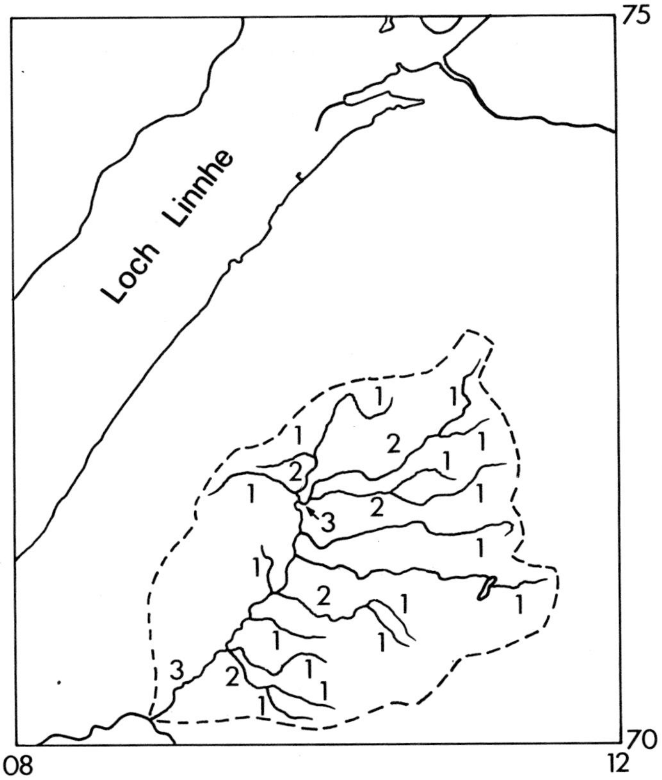

Fig. 20b Third order basin – Fort William map.

the work of rivers in the landscape. Selected measurements from the basins illustrated in Figs. 20a and 20b are set out in the table below.

Fig. 20a

Stream order	*No. of channels*	*Sum of channel lengths*	*Average channel length*	*Bifurcation ratio*
1	22	12.575	0.57	2.75
2	8	6.425	0.80	2.00
3	4	4.775	1.19	4.00
4	1	1.930	1.93	
Drainage basin	35	25.705	0.73	2.92

Fig. 20b

1	16	11.8	0.74	3.2
2	5	3.4	0.68	5.0
3	1	2.15	2.15	1.0
Drainage basin	22	17.35	0.79	3.07

The bifurcation ratio is the ratio of the number of stream segments of one order to those of the next highest order, i.e.

$$\text{Bifurcation ratio (Rb)} = \frac{\text{no. of streams of one order } (n)}{\text{no. of streams of next highest order } (n+1)}$$

and the mean, or average, bifurcation ratio for the basin as a whole is determined in the same way, e.g. for Fig. 20a:

$$\text{Basin Rb} = \frac{\frac{22}{8} + \frac{8}{4} + \frac{4}{1}}{3} = 2.92$$

It is also possible to work out the **drainage density** of the basin and this gives an indication of **terrain** texture, or the degree of dissection and differences in geological structure and/or lithology. It is necessary first to calculate the area of the basin (page 11) and to divide this into the total length of all stream segments, thus:

$$\text{Drainage density (Dd)} = \frac{\text{sum of channel lengths in kilometres}}{\text{area of basin in square kilometres}}$$

For the drainage basin illustrated in Fig. 20b from the Fort William map the Dd is:

$$\text{Dd} = \frac{\text{kilometres}}{\text{kilometres}^2} = \frac{17.35}{4.67} = 3.71$$

a

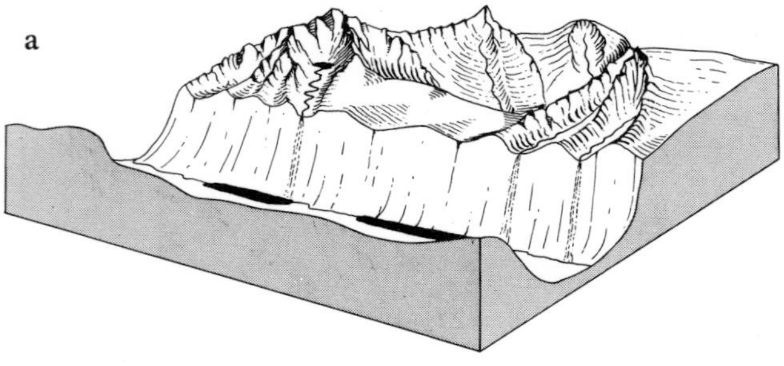

b

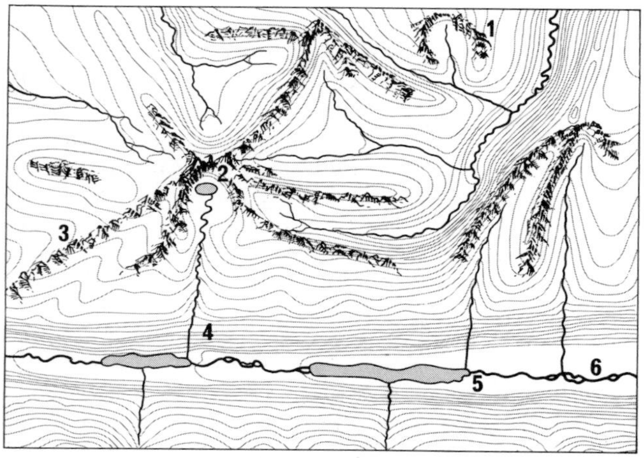

1. Corrie or cwm.
2. Corrie with tarn and pyramidal peak.
3. Arête.
4. Hanging valley waterfall.
5. Glacial lake.
6. Braided, misfit stream in U-shaped valley.

Fig. 21a and 21b Glaciated highlands.

Glaciated highlands

Many of the valleys of the Lake District, North Wales and Scotland and other mountainous regions cannot be explained by the work of rivers that flow through them today. They have been caused by the erosion of the valley glaciers which occupied them during the Ice Age. The sides of the valleys are steep and the former **spurs truncated**; the valley floor is broad and contains a **mis-fit river**; the V-shaped river valley has become a **U-shaped glaciated valley**. Above the valley sides we may find **hanging valleys** leading back to armchair-shaped hollows or **corries** (cwms) sometimes occupied by small lakes or **tarns**. When the corrie walls form narrow, angular ridges or edges they are called **arêtes** and they may converge in a single **summit** or **peak**. Excellent examples can be picked out on the Cairngorms map (Map 7), where the main valleys have been over-deepened and are occupied by lakes. The principal features of glaciated highlands are drawn on the block diagram and map—Figs. 21a and 21b.

a

b

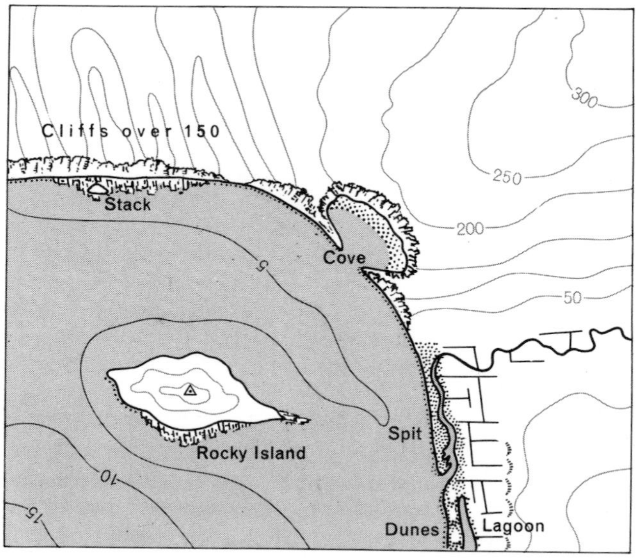

Fig. 22a and 22b Coastal forms.

Coastal forms

The insular nature of the British Isles means that many of the Ordnance Survey Maps are coastal sheets and demonstrate a great variety of coastal scenery. The special Ordnance Survey symbols for **cliffs**, **sand**, **shingle** and **marsh** indicate the nature of the coastline. The lines on the map showing the Ordinary limits of High and Low Water reveal the width of the Shore Zone and the symbols for sand, mud and shingle indicate the **type of beach**. High tidal waters may extend well up river valleys, particularly in the **drowned estuaries** or **rias** of south-west England and South Wales and suggest thereby how far inland the river is navigable.

Fathom lines indicate the depth of off-shore waters; in deep water wind-driven waves attack outstanding **headlands**, creating cliffs, small **peninsulas**, **caves**, **stacks** and natural arches and they drift the broken rock as sand and shingle into the shallower **bays** and along lowland coasts. At a river mouth or marked bend in the coastline this material might be drifted to form **shingle** and **sand spits** or bay-bars from headland to headland. Study these coastal forms on the map of Tenby (Map 2). The more common features are illustrated in the map and diagram, Figs. 22a and 22b.

Chapter five The identification of rock types

The topographical map usually provides some identifiable features that suggest the nature of the underlying rock. But lest the inexperienced map reader rushes in with hasty conclusions, where many experienced geographers and geologists fear to tread, a few words of warning must first be given. Quite commonly what appears as the clearest map evidence about rock type can be most misleading. On the 1:25,000 map of Ingleborough (but not on the 1:50,000 extract in this book) the words 'Granite Quarries' are written but the geologist would recognise the rock on field examination as arkose—a hard rock with the appearance and some of the properties of granite. No doubt it is quarried for road-building material and rough stone work, where granite might otherwise be used. Similarly 'Upper Slatepits' (106319) on the Cotswolds map (Map 4) is no certain sign that slate is dug at this place; without any doubt it is not the grey or green slate that has been used extensively throughout the country as a roofing material, although it is possible that the rock in this part of the Cotswolds would split into thin slabs suitable for covering roofing timbers. Place-names unsupported by other evidence can lead to wrong conclusions, for instance, 'White Hill Farm' may have no connection with limestone outcrops; in reality, it may describe nothing more than lime-washed cottages. The term 'Downs' is frequently used as evidence of chalk landscapes, but this word occurs over a wide range of rocks to describe a range of low hills.

Nevertheless, by assembling different pieces of map evidence—the types of land form, the pattern of drainage, mineral workings, vegetation pattern, land use and place-names—we can often come to a tentative conclusion about the nature of the underlying rock strata. We should never make an assumption about the rocks on the basis of only one piece of evidence. Certainly the existence of quarries, clay-pits and brick-fields, lime-workings and cement works, etc. may well confirm one's deductions drawn from other facts. An elementary knowledge of the characteristics of common rocks and the land forms associated with them will often provide the most significant data in the interpretation of the physical landscape.

Some rocks are resistant to the forces of erosion and stand high in the landscape as mountains or hills; others are weak and more rapidly removed by the action of rivers, ice and the waves of the sea to form vales, valleys and bays. Where the rocks are broken by many joints and fissures and the rock minerals are soluble in the percolating ground-water, the drainage may quickly pass underground and the map will show a dry landscape with few surface streams. Such rocks are said to be *permeable*. On the other hand, where the map shows abundant surface streams, tributaries joining rivers, perhaps across ill-drained land, the rocks are largely *impermeable*.

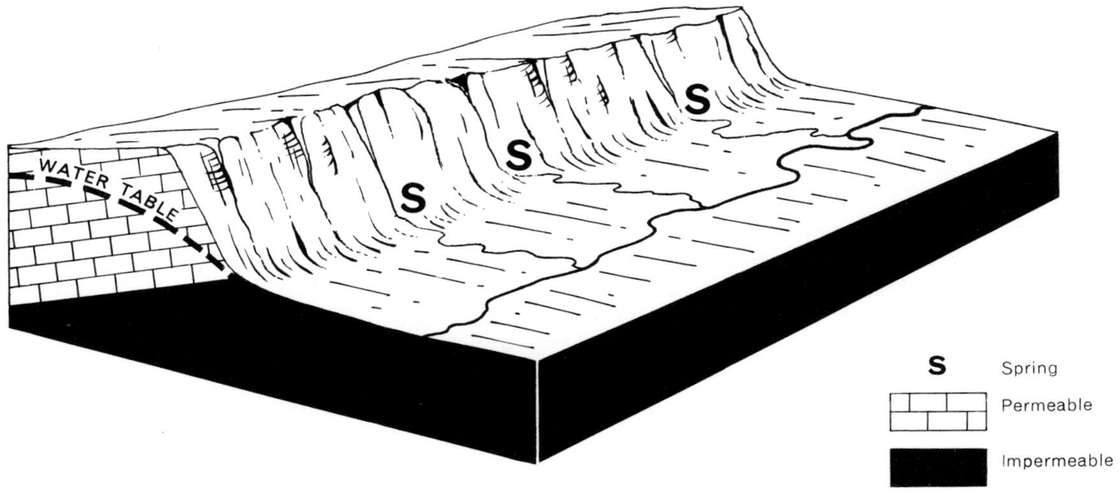

Fig. 23 The water table. At the junction of permeable and impermeable strata springs are usually found.

The permeable rocks

Rocks can be called permeable when, in humid regions there is little evidence of surface water. Their permeability may be due to a number of factors: to porosity—e.g. in some sandstones; to solubility—e.g. in limestones and those sandstones held together by lime cement; and to the extent to which rocks are broken by systems of joints and fissures. All these factors may be working together in varying degrees. The underground water moves along joint planes and fissure lines to emerge at spring heads where relatively impermeable rocks outcrop, so that a line of springs indicates generally the junction between permeable and impermeable rock strata. Such a junction might reveal the division between major rock types—e.g. between clay and limestone or it might indicate simply a band of rock within the limestone or sandstone series. The upper limit of the underground water is called the water-table, and this is shown in Fig. 23 in connection with the occurrence of springs.

Limestones

All rocks containing a high proportion of calcium carbonate are called limestones. In Britain the principal formations are:

(1) The crystalline limestones, largely of Carboniferous age which forms upland country, e.g. in the Craven District of the Yorkshire Pennines and in Derbyshire, the Mendips and parts of South Wales.

(2) The Jurassic limestones mainly oolitic in composition evident in the scarplands of the Midlands, the Cotswolds and the Hambleton Hills of north-east Yorkshire.

(3) The chalk, forming downland country in southern and eastern England.

The Carboniferous Limestone

This rock is highly permeable, the surface water disappearing below ground characteristically in small depressions known in England as 'pot-holes' or 'swallow-holes'. The pot-holes are often given local names and can be identified at once on the map, e.g. Gaping Gill Hole (751727) on the Ingleborough map (Map 6). In these regions the rock is strong enough to support caves in which the lime-charged waters deposit stalactites and stalagmites. The underground features cannot, of course, be portrayed on the map but because of their considerable interest to tourists they are frequently named on the map as: 'Caves', 'Passages', 'Water Swallows', etc. The higher slopes of the crystalline limestone may be broken by outcrops of bare rock, weathered into smooth blocks separated by shallow V-shaped depressions, the whole forming a fretted pavement of broken rock, called in Yorkshire clint and grike formation.

A characteristic feature is the valley once containing water, but now dry, which may terminate abruptly in a pot-hole. Several pot-holes may occur at intervals along the dry valley floors to be filled only after a heavy storm. Occasionally dry gorges may be found, for example, at Cheddar in the Mendips, and at the Winnats Pass near Castleton in Derbyshire. When the features are widespread the term 'karst' is applied to them, the name deriving from a large area of limestone scenery in north-west Yugoslavia.

In Part III of this book a detailed account of the limestones country around Ingleborough in the central Pennines will be found. This should be studied carefully and the exercises completed.

The Jurassic limestones

These limestones form ranges of hills running from north Yorkshire through the Midlands to Portland Bill and exhibit a great variety of land forms, so that generalisation is very difficult. They form a typical escarpment in the Cotswolds, where the rocks have a moderate dip to the south-east. In north-east Yorkshire the angle of dip is much less so that the land form is that of a dissected plateau. More surface drainage is usually found in these regions than in chalk landscapes as the limestone may contain a fair proportion of clay and clay bands outcrop in some places. However, good examples of dry valleys can be found, particularly in the Cotswolds, though the complete dry valley systems of chalk regions are generally absent. The Cotswolds scarp face shows considerable dissection into hollows or coombes and we may find patches of woodland known locally as 'hangers' clinging to the upper slopes. Good examples are seen on the map extract of this region in Part III. (Map 4).

Bands of ironstone occur interbedded with the limestone and are of economic importance at Corby in Northamptonshire and Scunthorpe in Lincolnshire. In the Cleveland Hills of north Yorkshire the ironstone is now almost exhausted. The map should reveal these iron workings; using opencast methods they cover large areas.

The admixture of clay and limestone has produced a good soil in many regions of this type and settlements are more closely distributed than in the chalk and crystalline limestones regions. On the Lincolnshire Edge the land is used for arable farming right along the crest of the escarpment.

The chalk

Although chalk is very permeable owing to its high porosity, the rock is mechanically weak and rarely supports caves. Pot-holes are absent though occasional small 'sinks' may be noted on the map. This rock is the well known scarp-former of the North and South Downs and the Chilterns, the relatively steep scarp face often cut into coombes and the gentle back or dip slope dissected by dry valleys. Here the valley forms are complex with major valleys joined by many tributary valleys increasing in width down the back slope until the water-table appears at the surface. The valleys are steep-sided and their floors rounded as though by running water. After an unusual period of heavy rain the water-table may rise and rivers flow, albeit temporarily in these valley courses. Such temporary streams are called 'bournes', 'winterbournes' or 'lavants', and the place-name 'bourne' is found frequently in chalk regions. At the base of the scarp slope streams issue from springs and flow across the clay lands in vales.

The hills are generally lower than in the Carboniferous Limestone regions and the rounded undulating outline of the chalk contrasts quite markedly with the angular sides and plateau summits of the harder limestone.

The natural vegetation of chalk lands is an open woodland of oak, hornbeam and beech with short turf, suitable for sheep grazing, but in recent years as farming techniques have changed, arable farming has extended over many former open pastures. A relic of the once extensive sheep farming on chalk and downland is the dew-pond. This is a small depression, either natural or man-made, lined with clay or floored with cement to collect rainwater for the watering of livestock. They are clearly distinguishable in blue on the 1:50,000 and 1:25,000 maps.

Today many are disused as the number of sheep has declined, and, in places they have been replaced by cisterns drawing water from underground sources by means of pipes.

Other evidence that may help in confirming a diagnosis of chalk includes: the frequency of the use of the words 'Downs' and 'Chalk' in place-names; the occurrence of white hill-figures ancient and modern; cement-works; and numerous antiquities, such as camps, tumuli and earthworks; for these more open areas were amongst the first settled by prehistoric man in Britain. But not one of these features by itself, should be considered of sufficient value to conclude that the land shown on any map is chalk country. Map 5 of part of the North Downs in the Hollingbourne area shows a typical chalk landscape of southern England.

The sandstones

Those sandstone rocks that are cemented by lime or are loosely consolidated are frequently permeable, and dry valleys may be seen on the map. They occur chiefly in lowland Britain (south and east of the Tees–Exe line) in the Greensand belts of the Weald of south-east England, at Sandringham, and in the glacial sands of the Breckland of Norfolk. The sandstone may form low ridges or ranges of hills, rising even to almost 300 metres above sea-level at Leith Hill in the western Weald. Sands and sandstone for building purposes are much in demand and the O.S. symbol for sand pits can usually be found on the map. Further evidence is often forthcoming in the symbols used for vegetation. The dry, acid soils of sandy regions support heath of gorse, broom and heather, and the O.S. maps distinguish the type of vegetation. Coniferous trees tolerate sandy habitats and in the lowland area if the tree symbols change from mixed or deciduous to coniferous woodland it is usually a good indication of a sandstone outcrop. Similarly, recent afforestation in lowland areas may be located on the poorer sandy soils, e.g. the Thetford and Brandon forests in Norfolk, and golf courses take advantage of the open undulating heaths. Finally, place-name evidence is almost certain to be seen in Sandpit Hill, Sand Gate Farm, the Sandlings, etc.

The impermeable rocks

Rocks are impermeable when they do not allow the free downward passage of water. This impermeability may be due to the closeness or absence of jointing which prevents the development of large open cracks in the rock, to the insoluble nature of the rock minerals or, as with clays, to the minute pore spaces that readily fill with water and prevent free circulation. Where these rocks outcrop at the surface, stream courses are everywhere evident and the land may be marshy and badly drained. Where the impermeable rocks outcrop below permeable strata they bring the water-table to the surface, and springs appear on the map. Impermeable rocks form both upland or lowland country.

The clays

Many kinds of clay of various geological ages occur in Britain, and as weak rocks, easily worn down by the forces of weathering and erosion, they form open vales, e.g. the Jurassic clay plains of Oxfordshire and Bedfordshire, and the Gault Clay of the Vale of Holmesdale at the foot of the North Downs in Kent. Clay is highly porous but very impermeable, and the heavy soils that develop on this rock may require extensive drainage before cultivation is possible. Consequently, map evidence will include straightened water-courses and artificial drainage cuts shown by thin blue lines.

Most of the major rivers of this country occupy these clay vales lying beyond the scarps of lowland England. These rivers, for example, the Thames, Great Ouse and Trent, may be seen on the map flowing slowly across the vales in wide-sweeping meanders, collecting tributary drainage on their way to the sea. These clay regions were formerly forested with damp oak-woods, and here and there patches of deciduous woodland can still be seen.

In East Anglia, parts of Lincolnshire and east Yorkshire, boulder clay was dumped by the ice sheets of the last Ice Age and masks the underlying chalk. It gives rise to small dissected plateaus with perched water-tables and belts of trees amidst rich farmland that has been trenched with tile field drains and is today intensively cultivated.

Map evidence of numerous brickyards and clay-pits is a sure sign of a clay outcrop; the old pits may be picked out, now filled with water as small ponds. Note that all badly drained land does not signify an outcrop of clay rock for the O.S. marsh symbol by river banks and around the mouths of estuaries portrays the superficial alluvium deposited by the river.

The sandstones

We have seen that some British sandstones are permeable but others are highly impermeable, such as the coarse Millstone Grit of the Pennines and the Pennant Sandstones of South Wales. These rocks are resistant and form wet, boggy moorland of heather, bilberry and cotton grass drained by innumerable streams locally named 'cloughs', 'gills' and 'becks'. In these regions surface water is abundant and the rainfall usually high so that open reservoirs can be constructed to supply with soft water, centres of population and industry, often many miles away.

The sides of the moor will be cut into steep-sided valleys as the rivers flow swiftly to adjacent lowlands. Wherever a harder band of rock outcrops, small waterfalls and rapids will be seen.

The rock may provide excellent building material, particularly the flagstones of the Pennines, and numerous quarries attest the heavy demand for this rock in the construction of the long dry stone walls separating Pennine fields and the buildings of the industrial north of England.

In Scotland and part of south-west England the Old Red Sandstone has long resisted the attacks of running water, ice and wind, and stands boldly in the landscapes, rounded in general outline as mountain or plateau.

Igneous and metamorphic rocks

A very great variety of these rocks is seen in western Britain from Devon and Cornwall to Scotland. Generally, the rocks are very impermeable, particularly the metamorphic slates, and in these regions of heavy rainfall surface water is abundant. Land forms developed in these rocks show an infinite variety and include the frost-shattered gabbro pinnacles of the Black Cuillins in Skye, the rounded slate summits of Skiddaw in the Lake District and the granite plateaus of Dartmoor and Bodmin Moor in south-west England. Some indication of rock type may be gleaned from named quarries on the map, and the Cornish granites are frequently associated with old mineral workings of veins of tin and arsenic and kaolin or china clay. But it would be foolhardy to attempt to draw conclusive evidence of these rock types solely from map evidence. Corroboration from a geological map would be essential.

In Part III the Cairngorms map (Map 7) shows mountains built of both igneous rock and schist; the Alloa sheet (Map 9) shows highlands formed of igneous rock material whilst shale underlies the area around Tenby (Map 2) and much of the upland country about Fort William is of metamorphic rock.

The Fenlands

Bordering the Wash of eastern England and in the lower course of the river Axe and neighbouring rivers in the West Country of Somerset are flat lands lying below the 15 metre contour. These regions were covered by water, both marine and fresh, when the sea-level stood higher than it does today. In the waters peat accumulated so that as the sea-level fell there was revealed a broad expanse of marshland with fen vegetation of reeds and willows growing alongside the streams and rivers. The natural fenland was a waste of reed and water at the level of the general water-table, but for centuries the land has been reclaimed by an intricate system of drainage channels. Today a map of the Fens shows a multiplicity of artificial drainage cuts. In eastern England the drains are integrated into a network of field drains flowing into dykes which in turn flow into main arterial drains or 'levels'. An excellent example of this type of country is seen in the map extract of the Middle Level of the Fens given in Part III (Map 2).

The principal characteristics that distinguish fenland from the marshland developed on clay rocks include the following: the overall level nature of the land; the low elevation, only a few metres above and occasionally even below sea-level; the long straight channels of the major drains embarked throughout their courses; the natural embankments of the rivers, often strengthened to prevent flooding, that have been built up above the general level of the shrinking cultivated fields; pumping stations to raise the water from one level to another; 'washes' of open pastures designed to take excess water in time of flood; a rectilinear pattern of roads leading to minor droves and following the drains, alongside which are isolated farms; and the frequent occurrence of the place-name 'fen'. On the small area of the 1:50,000 map extract referred to earlier, the word 'fen' appears six times. Villages are seen to be sited on slightly raised ground, small 'islands', that avoid the wet marshes.

Because the straight drainage ditches form the boundaries of the fields, the pattern of farm and field is very regular and geometrical, unlike the patchwork so often found elsewhere in the British Isles. As the price of land is very high because of its fertility and the costs of drainage, the size of the farm holding tends to be smaller than the average for the rest of the country; hence the density of farms is high.

In the Somerset fenland the word 'moor' is a misnomer, used to describe these lowlands. The correct word 'fen' is generally absent. Nor do we find in this smaller area the pattern of minor and major drains and pumping stations associated with the fenland around the Wash. Nevertheless the map should reveal the characteristic physical features of typical fenland. Other areas of fenland are to be seen in north Lincolnshire and across the Humber in Holderness.

Chapter six Types of settlement

By the time of the Domesday Book record of 1086 it is clear that the general pattern of settlement in England had been established. The Anglo-Saxon and later Scandinavian settlement had brought the small, compact village to the English plain. Some villages decayed, and were lost for centuries, to be discovered only in recent years by the archaeologist and historian. But the majority survived; some grew into towns and even cities as geographical conditions changed; others, less favoured, remained as villages, preserving even today the Anglo-Saxon grouping of farms and dwelling houses and the strip cultivation of the medieval open fields. Notable examples are the villages of Haxey, Lincolnshire, and Laxton, Nottingham. With the exception of a few settlements founded as industrial sites or holiday resorts all the villages and towns on the map put down their roots over 1,000 years ago. These villages were seldom founded by chance. The immigrant and invader chose a site possessing natural advantages over surrounding locations. We should be able to find out from the map evidence the nature of these advantages, and give some reason why one site was chosen rather than another. In the course of time roads, and very much later, railways, linked most of these settlements so that a convergence of routes on all larger settlements is characteristic. We must remember that in this sense all towns are **nodal towns**, roads converging on a point, or node, but this is in consequence of the important position of the town and not the cause of it. It is true, however, that recent growth around an old-established site may be due to its command over road and rail routeways, as in the **gap towns** of Lincoln and Leeds and the **rail junctions** at Crewe and Swindon.

Rarely do we find that a village owes its location to simply one natural advantage but several geographical factors combine and we may distinguish in any settlement the factor of **site**, **situation** and **function**.

Site

This is the building site, the actual area of land on which the settlement stands. It may be flat and permit the easy construction of dwellings; it may be elevated above the floodplains of a river nearby and thus avoid the danger of flooding, yet have ready access to water supplies. The **shape** of the site is important, providing clues to the way in which the settlement has grown. Thus the shape may be **nucleated**, i.e. around a marked centre such as a village green, a market, a church or a castle; or it may have a **linear** shape as in a street-village.

Situation

The situation or position of the settlement is its relationship with surrounding land and water features. It is its geographical setting. We have seen in Chapter 5 how springs occur at the junction of permeable and impermeable rocks at the foot of the scarp slope of limestone hills and at the edge of a clay vale. This is a common situation for a **water-seeking settlement**, but other advantages are usually also there. Thus the place avoids the wetter conditions of the clay vale and the steep slopes of the scarp face. Moreover the site may be sheltered from prevailing winds and in a favourable position for the exchange of goods produced in dissimilar geographical regions. The **fen-line villages** of Cambridgeshire occur around a spring-head below the scarp of the East Anglian Heights at the edge of the fen, where the fish, fowl and reeds of the fenland were exchanged for the farm produce of the upland.

Function

The principal function of a town may be immediately recognisable on the map from its situation and from name evidence—e.g. commercial ports, seaside holiday resorts, coal-mining centres. But, apart from natural route-centre functions performed by most towns it may be difficult to say from the map evidence anything about a town's present activities, particularly since towns today fulfil several functions. Some of these would include; **Ports—commercial, fishing, ferry or packet stations; resorts and dormitory towns; mining and other centres of mineral extraction; centres of heavy industry and manufacturing towns and cities; market towns and centres of local government administration.**

Upland settlements

In prehistoric and early historic times the lowlands of Britain were well-forested land or ill-drained marsh, so that man's first routes were the ridgeways across the more open uplands. With a few exceptions where these trackways led to the coast or crossed a river valley all the earliest settlements were on **hill-tops**, along recognised trade routes and in commanding positions, providing defence from attack. The O.S. map shows clearly these antiquities in Medieval style of printing as: Celtic fields; Entrenchments; Hill fort; Tumuli (Burial Mounds). 'Celtic Fields' indicates a site cultivated and settled for some time, but other sites may have been very temporary camps and defence-works. Although some of these locations were later taken over and built on by Roman invaders and even by Norman conquerors few have survived to the present day. Examples of prehistoric settlements now abandoned are Old Sarum near Salisbury, the British Camp on the Malvern Hills and Maiden Castle near Dorchester.

Roman settlements are shown in Roman capitals as: VILLA, CAMP, and the antiquities dating from A.D. 420 (when the Romans began to leave Britain) are also shown in Medieval type on the modern map editions. By the time of the Roman conquest settlements had spread to the valleys and vales as the woodland was slowly cleared. Upland settlement today includes **small nucleated villages** in sheltered positions around available water supplies, but few towns are seen. Alston in the northern Pennines of Cumberland, claiming to be the highest market town in England at 305 metres, has a population of only 1,900 (1978). For the rest, settlements are dispersed, the density of farms and other dwellings depending on the fertility of the soil, or the chance outcrop of rocks suitable for quarrying; or special factors such as Princeton on Dartmoor, supported by the prison.

Lowland settlements

Man is essentially a lowlander and it is in the broad open vales and river valleys that our major towns and cities have grown. According to the principal geographical advantages of each one we can distinguish several types of settlement.

Confluence towns

Where two or three rivers meet and the valley routes converge we find the confluence town. It may also have a market function or operate as a river port.

Examples

Reading, Salisbury, Oxford, Tewkesbury and Monmouth. See Fig. 25.

Market towns

These are centrally situated in the areas they serve, their advantages of position causing them to grow at the expense of surrounding settlements. Because of their greater importance, roads and railways converge on them, emphasising their nodal situations.

Examples

Figure 26, Melton Mowbray, Bedford, Taunton, Hereford, and most other county towns.

Foot-hill settlements

Villages have developed at the junction of lowland and upland where the hills afforded shelter from rough weather and the plain provided ease of communication. The settlements are frequently found where a river has cut through the hills giving access to higher ground. Spring-line settlements are also of this type.

Examples

The spring-line and fen-line settlements mentioned above; settlements in the Vale of Strathmore at the foot of the Grampian Mountains and in the Vale of Pickering at the foothills of the North York Moors. See also Map 9 and Fig. 27.

Gap towns

Road and railways converge to pass through a natural gap, usually cut by a river in a range of hills, thus providing the easiest route across the upland. A settlement in the gap will benefit from the traffic passing through it and many towns of this type can be found throughout the British Isles. Close examination of the gap may reveal the ancient nucleus around a castle or old fortification overlooking the gap, as at Lewes, Arundel and Lincoln. We should remember that the early importance of the gaps was due not to the routes through the valleys but to the ridgeways which were compelled to descend the valley slopes at these places.

Examples

Figure 28, Goring-on-Thames; the towns controlling routes through the North and South Downs and the Chilterns where paired gap towns may be found at the foot of both scarp and dip slopes, e.g. Leatherhead and Dorking; Princes Risborough and High Wycombe. Others include Hexham (Tyne Gap); Skipton (Aire Gap); Stirling and Perth (in gaps cut by the Forth and Tay between the Sidlaws, Ochils and Campsie Fells).

Dry-point sites

On higher ground around marshes and along the floodplains of rivers, settlements avoided waterlogged conditions arising from the flooding of rivers at times of high tidal water and storm. The **fen-line villages** of Lincolnshire, Cambridgeshire and Norfolk referred to above, and the **clay and gravel islands** rising above the level of the undrained Fens are on dry-point sites.

Examples

Downham Market (Map 3), Ely, March, Ramsey, Cheddar, Wells, and see also Figs. 24a and 24b.

Wet-point sites

Villages were founded around wells and springs where a pure and regular water supply was at hand. Such settlements are commonly found at the base of the scarp slope of limestone hills (see p. 56) strung out along a natural line at the spring-head. These are called **spring-line settlements**. They may also occur at the base of the dip or back slope.

Examples

At the base of Chalk escarpments of the South Downs, North Downs, Salisbury Plain, Lincoln Edge and the oolitic limestones of the Cotswolds and Northamptonshire uplands. See Fig. 29.

Fen island settlements

Early settlement in the lowlands around the Wash was made on small island sites above the surrounding marsh. These dry places provided a firm foundation for building and a refuge from flooding. Today the marsh has been drained and road and rail link the former islands to the neighbouring uplands. Haddenham, Wilburton and Sutton occupy low ridges between 15 metres and 30 metres and the surrounding fen in this area is near and in places below sea-level. The map shows that no new settlements have grown in the drained fen as the drying out has caused the peaty fen soil to shrink and this limits the construction of permanent dwellings. Thus the older island sites retain a greater importance as the only major settlements in the area.

Other examples of this type of settlement can be seen in the Levels of Somerset, formerly marshland which was drained about the same time as the Fens of eastern England, mainly under the direction of the same engineer, the Dutchman Cornelius Vermuyden. Island sites such as Glastonbury compare closely with Ely and the surrounding lowland shows similar features to the Fens with the straightened courses of the rivers Axe, Brue and Parrett and the dense network of field drains locally known as rhynes.

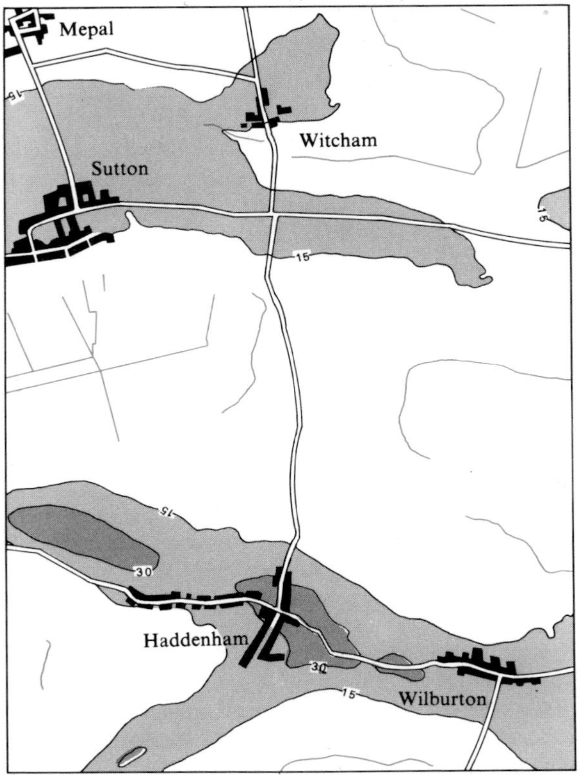

Fig. 24a Fen island settlement. Scale: 1:75,000

Fen-line settlement

The villages of Swaffham Prior, Swaffham Bulbeck and Burwell are representative of many settlements located at the junction of the fen and the upland. They occupy sites about 15 metres above sea-level and are raised slightly above the old marsh. These are the fen-line settlements. The sites are both water-shunning and water-seeking in that they avoid the damp fen, yet are located near freshwater springs. Many of these villages were formerly small fen ports, used by barges of shallow draught transporting the fish, reeds and wildfowl of the fen to exchange for the corn and meat of the uplands. Through the intricate waterways of the region they were connected to the larger seaports of the Wash.

A close study of parish boundary lines in the fen edge will usually show long narrow parishes running from the upland to the marsh. Within each parish the medieval villagers achieved some degree of self-sufficiency, summer grazing in the fen, good arable land at the scarp foot, a little timber from the hanger woods on the steeper slopes and building material by easy quarrying.

These maps jointly show a strip of country stretching to the north-west from the East Anglian Heights near Cambridge into the Middle Levels of the Fens. Compare with Map 3.

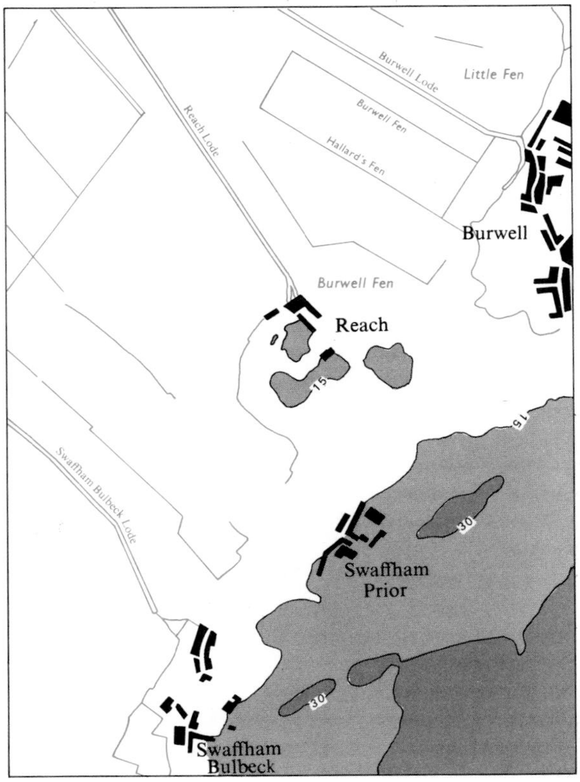

Fig. 24b Fen-line settlement. Scale: 1:75,000

Confluence town, Monmouth

This old county town is an example of the combination of several factors of site and situation.

(a) Confluence between the river Wye and its tributary, the Monnow, providing a small area of land suitable for building.
(b) Gap town and route centre where three valley ways and two ridge-ways converge.
(c) Defence site encompassed on three sides by water and high ground to the north. Monmouth was one of the most important towns along the Welsh Marches guarding the route to the west.
(d) Market centre served by major and minor roads and, until recently, by three branch line railways.

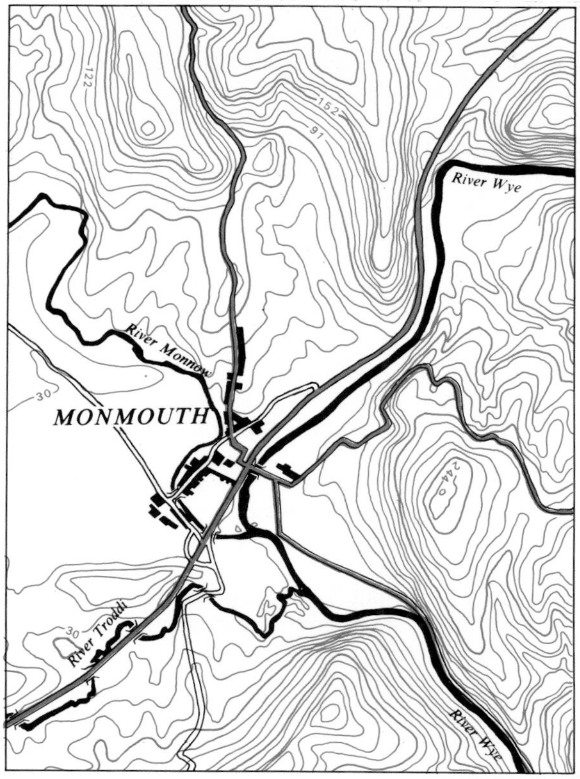

Fig. 25 Confluence town, Monmouth. Scale: 1:75,000

Market town, Melton Mowbray

Centrally situated in the rich dairy farming area of the Wreake Valley, Melton Mowbray is the focus of numerous roads and the crossing place of two main line railways. The east–west line, the old Midland and Great Northern, is now closed to passengers. The traditional market in butter, cheese, meat and other agricultural produce is today supplemented by food manufacturing industries and by some heavy industry on the Leicester iron-ore field. Many market towns have wide, high streets and squares with centrally situated corn exchanges, butter markets and wool halls. The detail of the larger scale maps should show this plan, a wide central area with public buildings in black.

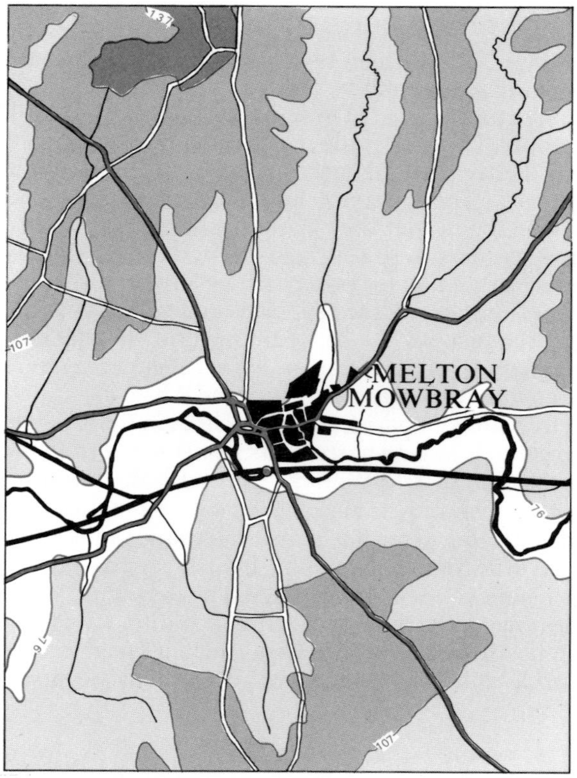

Fig. 26 Market town, Melton Mowbray. Scale: 1:75,000

Foot-hill settlement, Alva

The small town of Alva is situated at the foot of the Ochil Hills. The site lies above the flood plain of the river Devon between the 15 metre and 46 metre contours on a small platform where a tributary stream—the Alva Burn—leaves its restricted upland valley and enters the broader main valley. At the junction of upland and lowland the speed of the burn has been checked and Alva is probably sited on alluvium dropped there by the stream. The fast-flowing stream provided power and soft water for a small wool industry, using the local clip.

Compare with Map 9 and Plate 5 in Chapter 14.

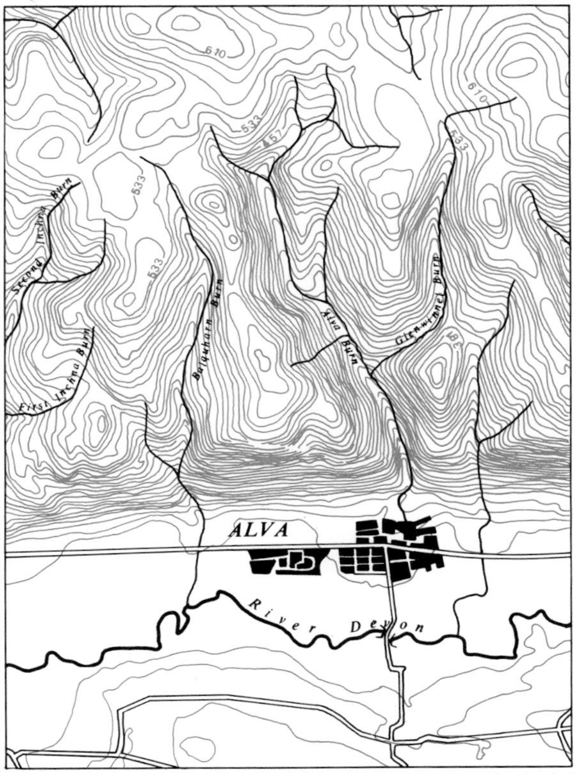

Fig. 27 Foot-hill settlement, Alva. Scale: 1:75,000

Gap town, Goring-on-Thames

In the narrow gap cut by the Thames between the Chilterns and Berkshire Downs, Goring and Pangbourne control the road and rail routes which link the London Basin in the south with the Oxford Clay Vale to the north. The through valley of the Thames is the only lowland gap in this part of the chalk escarpment. Other route-ways crossing the Chilterns make use of cols and must cross the scarp slope into the northern vale. The map shows two locks on the river Thames indicating that here there is a navigable waterway, although somewhat shallow. Traffic is confined to small barges and pleasure craft and Goring, therefore, shares in this trade.

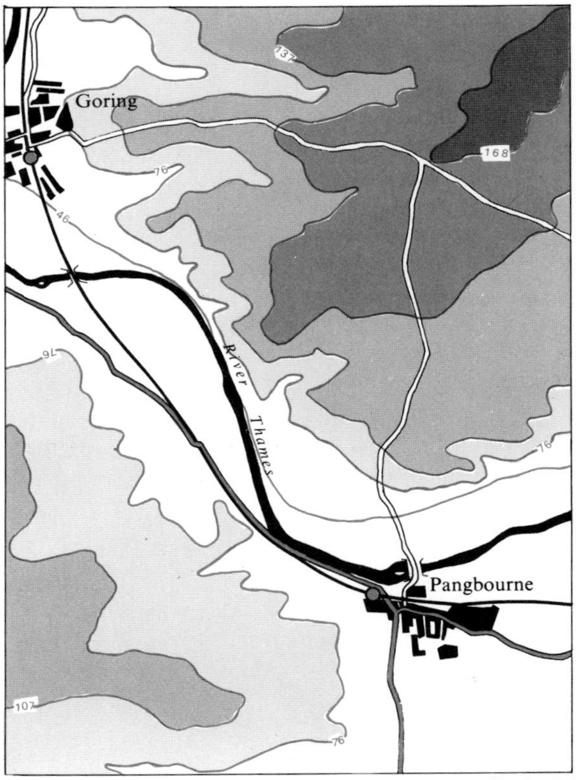

Fig. 28 Gap town: Goring-on-Thames Scale: 1:75,000

Spring-line settlement, Wiltshire

Spring-line settlement, Wiltshire. The villages of Compton Bassett and Cherhill, lie on or near the spring-line about 120 metres above sea-level at the foot of the scarp of the Marlborough Downs. Compare these sites with those shown on Fig 24b. Other than the supply of fresh water there were probably several other advantages of both site and situation. The position is sheltered in a dissected scarp face and at the break of slope building would not be too difficult and mixed soils offered some prospect for agriculture. This area of England saw some of the first farming by Neolithic peoples on the easily cleared higher slopes of the chalk upland. Later early medieval settlement spread to the present scarp foot sites.

Settlements in a similar position can be seen at the base of the limestone escarpment of the Cotswolds (Map 4).

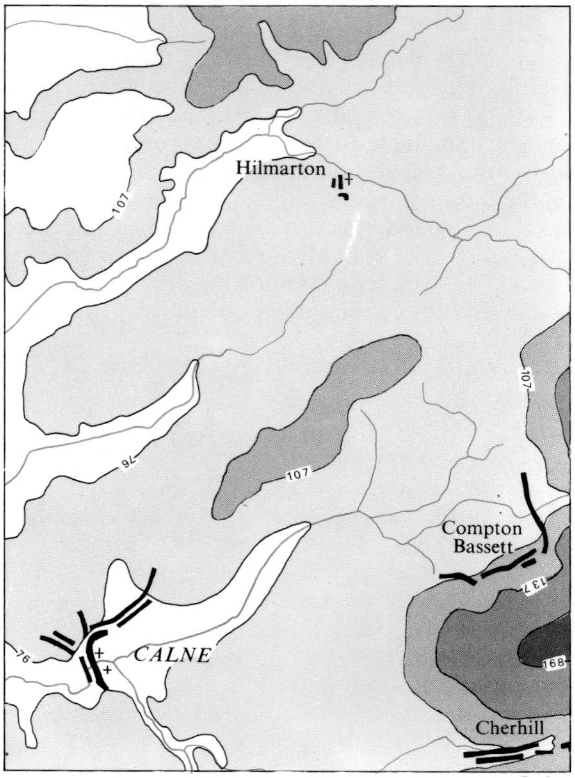

Fig. 29 Spring-line settlement, Wiltshire. Scale: 1:75,000

Bridge town, Bridgwater

Bridgwater in Somerset has grown up at a convenient crossing point on the river Parrett. Below the town the river was too wide for easy bridge construction so that coastal roads must turn inland to cross the river near the head of its estuary. Highbridge, on the river Brue, to the north, is another example of settlement located at the lowest bridging point. Both towns have the further advantage of being situated at the head of navigation of the rivers on which they stand. Other examples can be found well inland from the coast. Place-name evidence for the origin of the settlement may often be seen as in 'Cambridge' and 'Oxford'.

Today these old bridge towns are losing some of their importance as traffic is diverted to more direct routes over wide estuaries, such as the Forth, Severn and Tay. These new bridges carry modern highways and are unlikely to attract settlement of any kind.

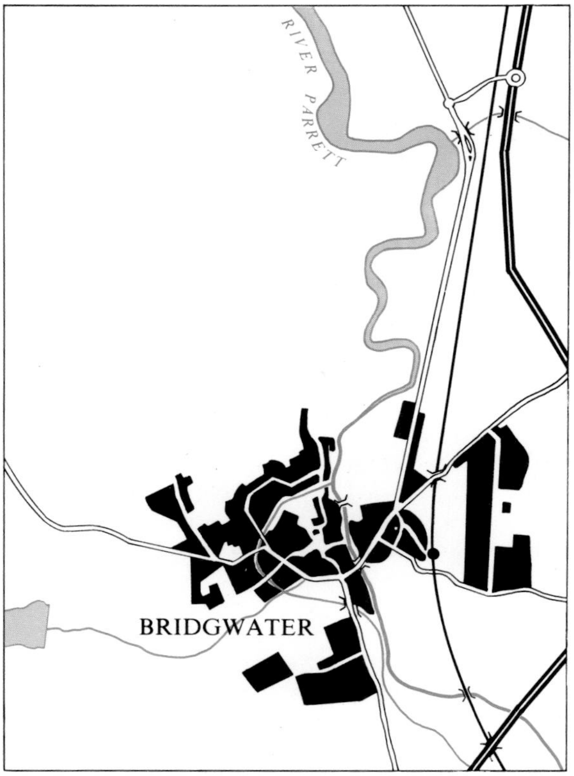

Fig. 30 Bridge town, Bridgwater.

Bridge towns

Wherever routes could cross a river or stream by a ford in early times and later by a bridge, the crossing-point often became the site of a settlement controlling the traffic. Not all bridge points attracted permanent settlement but particularly important was the lowest crossing-point on a river, below which the tidal waters of the estuary were too wide and turbulent for bridge construction.

Examples

Figure 30, Bridgwater; Alloa (Map 9); London; Lancaster; Stirling and Perth; Gloucester.

Industrial towns

The size of the larger towns and cities is generally dependent on their industrial activities, but these are not always evident on the map. We can only suggest reasons for the earliest settlement and not for later growth. An example of one of the few towns which grew around a single industry was at Skinningrove, in north-east Yorkshire.

Coastal settlements

The insular nature and long indented coastline of the British Isles have provided many advantageous sites for settlements. They fall into two groups—the ports and the resorts.

The ports

Commercial ports dealing in a great variety of trade and handling passenger traffic from the sea highways of the world have developed in deep sheltered estuaries away from the storms of the open sea. How far the deep-water estuary has influenced the building of the ports may be judged from the lines on the map showing the extent of High and Low Water. The larger ports will show a long waterfront site backed by warehouses, dry docks, shipbuilding yards, offices, refineries and factories and behind them are sited the shops and residential suburbs. A few ports in similar situations have specialised as **naval dockyards**, building and servicing the Royal Navy. As ships have grown in size and the heads of some estuaries have become choked with silt **outports** have been constructed near the mouths of certain estuaries to deal with the vessels of larger draught. Although most ports will have a small fleet, fishing inshore waters, the principal fleets of deep-sea fishing vessels come from specialised ports with large fish markets, freezing and canning industries, and good rail facilities for quick despatch to urban markets. Grimsby, the second largest **fishing port** in Britain, is highly specialised, dealing almost exclusively in fish. Facing the North Sea it is situated well down the Humber estuary. Of the smaller ports only a few retain an importance for fishing, e.g. Newlyn (Cornwall), Milford Haven (South Wales) and Whitby (Yorkshire).

Ferry ports or packet stations to the Continent, Ireland and the islands around our shores will show small dock facilities, sufficient to cater for passenger embarkation and to deal with mail. They have grown up at a river mouth or on a headland with good rail connections to the major cities inland.

Examples

Commercial and passenger ports. London; Liverpool; Glasgow; Southampton; Hull; Newcastle; Bristol; Belfast.
Outports. Avonmouth; Tilbury; Cobh (for Cork).
Naval bases. Portsmouth; Plymouth; Portland; Scapa Flow; Rosyth.
Fishing ports. Grimsby; Fleetwood; Aberdeen; Hull; Lowestoft.
Ferry ports. Dover; Folkstone; Newhaven; Tilbury; Harwich; Fishguard; Holyhead; Heysham; Weymouth; Stranraer and many other small ports serving the Scottish islands, e.g. Oban for Mull and Kyle of Lochalsh for Skye.

The resorts

Holiday resorts, **retiring-places** and **dormitory towns** are to be seen in great numbers along many stretches of the coast. Their present-day function may have largely replaced an older fishing or trading port—as Hastings, Southend and Great Yarmouth—as the tourist industry has expanded. The characteristic site shows ribbon development above the cliffs or along the promenades. Advantages of situation may include some or all of the following factors: a wide seashore with sand or shingle beach; southerly aspect; shelter from prevailing winds; variety of scenery on the coast and immediately inland; proximity to large centres of population. The map evidence will include a large residential area, well-laid-out parks, swimming-pools, a golf course, etc.

Examples

Aberystwyth, Oban, and many others should at once come to mind.

A few inland spas perform a similar function. Bath dates from Roman times but the other spas chiefly owe their importance to the eighteenth-century habit of 'taking the waters', e.g. at Tunbridge Wells, Leamington Spa, (Map 10) Cheltenham, Harrogate and Buxton.

Chapter seven Communications

We can imagine Man in the early civilisations of the Middle East drawing in the soil or sand and making the first maps. They would be route-maps, recording journeys and fixing important landmarks, and would be transferred later to stone tablets or papyrus. So, as the civilised world expanded the new cartographers would fill in details on maps and charts of these new routes overland and across the seas. In Britain the Romans produced itineraries, setting out distances along the great roads they built, and in the seventeenth century, a well known map-maker, John Ogilvie, constructed elaborate road-strip maps similar to those issued today by the motoring associations. But these were not maps in the true sense, as they simply recorded distances and paid little attention to scale; direction was largely ignored. On modern maps all forms of communications are shown and distances can be measured accurately in terms of the scale of the map.

Roads

The Ordnance Survey distinguish roads by their width and their surface. From the map symbols we can recognise fenced and unfenced roads, footpaths, trackways and the various roads classified by the Ministry of Transport, including the new Motorways.

Footpaths

These are found in open country and in the hills and mountains where construction of metalled road surfaces is unnecessary or impracticable. The prehistoric ridgeways can be distinguished from other footpaths and tracks by their accompanying tumuli and other antiquities. They are frequently named, e.g. the Icknield Way crossing the chalk downland of south-east Cambridgeshire. The military Roman roads can be seen by their straight stretches marching across the countryside, ignoring the contours, and by the ancient names of Watling Street, Ermine Street, Stane Street, etc.

The origin of the rolling English road probably can be found in the 'green roads' and cattle droves of the Middle Ages. It can be identified picking its way across the lowlands of Britain linking up ancient settlements, skirting the old field boundaries and avoiding marshland and steeply rising ground. In great contrast are the roads of recent date. They have the straight course of the old Roman roads negotiating wet land and hill-sides by embankments, cuttings and viaducts, to maintain a flat and level surface. Examples of the new roads should be sought on the relevant sheets of the O.S. maps—e.g. the improved sections of the A1 and the Motorway network, e.g. M1—London–Leeds; M4—London–Bristol and South Wales; M62 the trans-Pennine Motorway from Hull to Liverpool.

Rivers

Rivers must have been used from the earliest times as a way into the interior from the coast. The extent to which they are used today for communications can not always be discovered from the map. The location of various types of ports near the river mouth has been discussed in Chapter 6 (p. 37), but further upstream even beyond tidal influence, the river may act as a highway for small craft, such as barges and other motor boats. The occurrence of locks, towing paths, piers for unloading, straightened courses, dense building near the riverside will suggest this kind of use. The river Trent carries a considerable traffic as far inland as the Potteries. Although road and rail transport have taken away much of the river cargo some river ports are still important. They include Wisbech on the Nene, and Norwich on the river Wensum.

Canals

The majority of canals were dug in the eighteenth century to carry the bulk goods of the Industrial Revolution. We should expect to see them linking the old centres of heavy industry joining the navigable sections of rivers and leading to London and the seaports. Although much of this trade was quickly taken over by the railways, and many are today unused, they are immediately recognisable on a map. Note how, unlike rivers, they maintain long straight sections along the contours, moving from one level to another by means of locks. The coal-field centres of industry are found on the edge of the uplands and so great engineering skill was called for in the cutting of the canals. In the Midlands of England, across the Pennines between Yorkshire and Lancashire and on the Welsh border the map reveals the work of the canal builders—in the construction of aqueducts, embankments and locks, and in the digging of cuttings and canal tunnels. There should be no confusion between the waterways and rivers as seen on the map: the canals are named in blue, Grand Union Canal, Aire and Calder Canal, etc.

and a towing path for the horse-drawn barge runs alongside. Drainage channels which also follow a straight course are distinctively named, e.g. Middle Level Drain in the Fens (Map 3).

Railways

The nineteenth century was the great period of railway construction. Only in the very remote parts of Britain could one find a map with no section of railway track; in just over 100 years the railways were extended the length and breadth of the land. Like canal construction, railway construction was also controlled by relief. The lines seek out the river gaps and passes and maintain a level course by cuttings, bridges, viaducts and embankments. Where gradients were too steep for cuttings to be made tunnels were dug. The long tunnels across the Pennines—The Summit, Standedge and Woodhead tunnels—demonstrate how physical barriers were overcome.

On the O.S. map we can distinguish, by the symbols, between multiple and single tracks, small gauge and mineral working lines, and all the constructional detail is given alongside the track. These railways followed as direct a course as relief and land purchase permitted, joining up the larger centres of population, so that villages in non-industrial areas were often bypassed or the station built a short distance away. Today the greater volume of road traffic has compelled the railways to close unprofitable branch lines, many small stations and halts. The closed station is indicated by an open circle across the line. Many places were stimulated in their growth by the arrival of the railway and a few owe their present importance almost entirely to it. Crewe, Rugby, Swindon and Eastleigh are large junctions where the repair and manufacture of railway engines and rolling stock is carried out. The small town of Wolverton in Buckinghamshire was almost completely created as a wagon and repair centre.

Air communications

Because of the long runways required and the undesirable noise and danger of modern aircraft, airfields are at some distance away from the heavily built-up areas they serve. Thus the airports for London are many miles away from the city's centre at Heathrow, Gatwick and Southend. Aerodromes acting as passenger terminals are named on the map as 'Airports' and runways may be shown by broken lines; others for military and club use are simply marked 'Airfield'.

Description of a route

Examination questions on the subject of communications are generally of two kinds: (1) a description of a route along a footpath, river, road or railway; (2) the relationship between communications and the land and water features.

(1) Route description should keep to the area crossed by road, rail, etc. and the features close by. Do not describe distant prospects, but indicate the course taken by reference to distance, direction, elevation, slope, nature of land forms crossed; and to the surface and special features of construction, such as tunnels and level crossings, road junctions and bridges. An example of such a description is given below, taken from the Pershore map (Map 1)—Ufnell Bridge (930475) to Little Comberton (967430).

'The A44 leaves Ufnell Bridge in a southerly direction, but after 0.5 kilometre it bends to the south-east towards the small town of Pershore. The road climbs gradually from 21 metres above sea level to the 55-metre contour before descending a gentle slope through the town. A minor road joins the A44 from the west at 940463, and on the outskirts of Pershore the A4104 comes in from the south-west. The A44 then runs west to east just to the north of the central business area of the town and the B4083 takes traffic away to the north at this point. The main road then turns south-south-east through the built-up area near to the Market, Library and main Post Office towards the river Avon. The river is crossed by a new bridge, as the narrow old Pershore Bridge nearby is used today only by pedestrians. On reaching the east bank the A44 continues in an easterly direction but the Comberton road forks right, climbing for 0.25 kilometre, and then left at a minor road junction. In another 0.5 kilometre the road to Little Comberton turns left again to the south-east, drops to cross the Mary Brook and then rises gently over a distance of 1 kilometre to 32 metres above sea level in the centre of the village.'

(2) Relationship to relief and drainage. This type of question seeks information about the ways by which roads, railways and canals avoid steep gradients and the wet valley bottoms; how they approach bridging-points across a river, and negotiate hill ranges through gaps and passes.

We can now examine the same route on the Pershore map described above to illustrate the difference in the two approaches to route description, this time relating the road to the relief and drainage.

'Leaving Ufnell Bridge and the narrow valley of the Bow Brook, the A44 rises gently along the side of Allesborough Hill and drops from a height of 54 metres down a short hill to Pershore and southwards to the flood plain of the river Avon. A weir and lock control the river above the bridge-crossing at 15 metres above sea-level. The road then climbs obliquely across the steep river cliff before crossing a flat-topped ridge at 40 metres and then descends to cross the small Mary Brook at 19 metres above sea-level before rising 13 metres very gently over a distance of 1 kilometre to the centre of Little Comberton.'

Other examples of this kind of control are given in the map analyses in Part III. Note particularly the analysis of the Alloa sheet (Map 9).

Chapter eight Land use

How much can we discover from the map of the many different ways in which the earth's surface is used by Man? There is the direct evidence of actual buildings, a clear form of land use; and by names and symbols we can see other uses, such as mines, quarries, reservoirs, parkland, orchards and other semi-permanent features. But the farming use of land is not so permanent, changing as management and market conditions change, and so no indication of the type of farming is given. Special Land Use maps on a scale of 1:63,360 were published before the war, but these have now little more than historical interest. A new series of maps is being published on the 1:25,000 scale in the Second Land Utilisation Survey of Britain, directed by Alice Coleman, M.A., and at the present time (1979) a large selection of sheets is available. The information about land is overprinted in colours on the O.S. topographical map and each sheet corresponds to the New Series 1:25,000 Ordnance map. From the standard topographic map our interpretation of farming activities will be inferred from the nature of the land surface and its drainage, the density of farms and any special symbols employed.

Farming land use

A high density of farms may indicate a high fertility of soil and intensive farming. The close network of drains in the Fens (Map 3) suggest a rich soil yielding a high return to offset some of the heavy costs of drainage. Whether arable crops or pasture predominate cannot be told, but a knowledge of the economic geography of the country will enable us to make a calculated guess. Land under orchards is shown by a regularly spaced tree symbol and horticulture by a glasshouse device. In upland areas a rough grazing symbol is used on uncultivated land and we can safely conclude that the occasional farms rear flocks of sheep. Similarly, lowland marshes are more likely to be used for cattle grazing rather than for cultivation, although Romney Marsh is traditionally a sheep-grazing area.

Woodland

A distinction is drawn between coniferous, deciduous and mixed woodland by pictorial symbols. Afforested areas can usually be spotted as they are almost entirely of conifers and the boundary enclosures are more regular than those around natural forests and woods.

Mineral extraction

The quarry symbol locates the extraction of rocks such as building stone, ironstones, limestone and chalk; the open pit symbol indicates the loose diggings of sand and gravel. Underground extraction is seen by the word 'Mines', and this will usually mean coalmines today.

Industrial use

We must look for the functional arrangement of buildings around railway-sidings, quays, and some named evidence of industry, e.g. factory, mills, works, docks. The nature of the work is not given. From the shape of the buildings and such features as the small circles representing oil storage tanks and gas-holders, the presence of industry can be deduced.

Recreational use

In and around large centres of population and at the seaside, will be found parks, gardens, playing fields, golf courses, etc. In areas of great natural beauty we shall find the National Parks, Nature Reserves and National Trust Properties, and alongside stretches of water, such as the Norfolk Broads, we can expect to see mentioned the Sailing Club Houses and attendant boat and mooring yards.

Waste land

This can usually be inferred in areas of very high, badly drained land and on surfaces of broken rock such as the high mountains and moorlands of Britain. Similarly coastal dunes, mudflats and salt-marshes have very low economic value. Tip heaps and spoil heaps, the by-products of mining and heavy ore refining fall into this category although disused quarries may have some value for the dumping of public refuse.

Examples

Consult the relevant map-extracts.
Farming. Contrast Maps 1 and 2 with Maps 4 and 5.
Woodland. Maps 5 and 7—note distribution of natural woodland and afforestation.
Mineral Extraction and Industry. Maps 6 and 8.
Recreational. Compare evidence on Maps 2 and 8.
Waste Lands. Exposed and rock-strewn ground—Maps 6 and 7.

PART THREE ANALYSIS OF SELECTED MAPS AND MAP EXERCISES

Questions on Part Three

Pershore

Question paper 1—Map 1

1. Explain the meaning of the words Emp Ex in grid square 9446. Why is this function well located at this point?
2. Draw a sketch-map of all water features shown on the map extract and label one example of each of the following: flood-plain terrace; ait; under-cut river cliff; slip-off slope; levee.
3. How much shorter is the distance on foot between The Grange in Birlingham (935424) and the centre of Little Comberton village, than the shortest distance by motor road between the same places?
4. Describe, and suggest reasons for, the distribution of orchards east of the river Avon.

Question paper 2—Map 1

1. Describe the route taken by a small boat between the Locks at Pershore and Nafford. Confine your description to the river and the land immediately around it.
2. Suggest what might take place at Swan's Neck (930424) during times of heavy flood-water discharge.
3. Account for the routes taken by the A44 and A4104–B4083 across the map.
4. Draw a sketch-map to show the situation of Pershore.

Supplementary questions—Map 1

1. Why is there a Danger Area marked on the edge of Tyddesley Wood?
2. Place tracing paper over the entire map and mark on it all field boundaries. Divide the fields into three groups: large, medium, small, and shade accordingly. Attempt to explain the differences in the distribution of field sizes.
3. On a tracing of the built-up area of Pershore show, by appropriate shading: the core of the town; recent housing; industrial and commercial buildings.
4. Give three reasons to prove that the river Avon is flowing from north to south.

Tenby

Question paper 1—Map 2

1. Give grid references for one example of each of the following: a foot-bridge; life-boat station; National Trust property; railway viaduct.
2. Estimate to an accuracy of 0.5 square kilometre the area of sandy beach exposed at low water.
3. Describe in detail the appearance of the area if the mean sea-level were to rise by 10 metres.
4. Suggest reasons for the location of the harbour on the north side of the Tenby peninsula.

Question paper 2—Map 2

1. State the distance in kilometres, and the direction, between Giltar Point (125983) and Monkstone Point (148033).
2. Examine the photograph of Tenby, Plate 2, and state: the direction of flight of the aircraft; the season of the year; the time of day.
3. Use the map and the photograph, Plate 2 to prepare a plan, to the scale of 1:6250, of that part of the site of Tenby contained within grid square 1300.
4. Explain how the route followed by the railway is related to the physical features of the area.

Supplementary questions—Map 2

1. Suggest the ways by which the householders at Twy Cross and New Hedges are provided with water.
2. Prepare a sketch-map to show the communications network of the area.
3. By means of a cross-section determine whether the museum on Castle Hill at Tenby can be seen from the cross-roads at Twy Cross.
4. Attempt to explain the origin of The Burrows and South Beach between Penally and the Tenby peninsula.
5. Describe the landscape features seen on the walk by the Pembrokeshire Coast Path from Tenby to the northern edge of the map.
6. Explain the origin of the waterfalls along the north-east section of the coastline.

Fenland

Question paper 1—Map 3

1. Write an account of the drainage channels seen on the map under the headings: (a) natural water-courses; (b) field drains; (c) main drains.
2. Explain briefly the functions of the Sluice and Locks at 588010.
3. Describe the shape and site of the villages of Outwell and Nordelph.
4. Suggest reasons for the growth of the settlement at Downham Market.

Question paper 2—Map 3

1. On a sketch-map of the area given on the map extract indicate clearly the following: 15-metre contour line; the river Ouse; the Middle Level Main Drain; three sites close to sea-level; a section of a narrow-gauge railway; a disused windmill probably used formerly for pumping.
2. On an enlarged sketch-map show all the drainage features and flood control on the river Ouse between Denver Sluice and Downham Bridge.
3. Attempt to account for the growth of the villages of Hilgay, Denver and Wimbotsham.
4. Outline the map evidence that suggests that this is an important farming area.

Supplementary questions—Map 3

1. List three pieces of map evidence that clearly reveal that most of the land shown on the map is about sea-level.
2. Indicate any difficulties likely to arise in the farming of Stow Bardolph Fen.
3. Describe the course of the A1122 from Scott's Bridge to Salter's Lode.
4. Suggest reasons why the B1094 no longer follows the course of the Roman Road.
5. Why would you consider that the settlement at Hilgay is older than that at Barroway Drove?
6. Using the vertical air photograph, Plate 3, and the map state by means of six-figure grid references the locations of points A, B and C marked on the photograph.
7. Explain the differences between the water-courses flowing to the Great Ouse river from Fordham and Hilgay.
8. Give reasons why most of the fields around the village of Outwell are smaller than those in the rest of the fen.
9. The additional information on the photograph confirms that this area is one of intensive arable farming. List the evidence in support of this statement.
10. By careful measurement on both map and photograph calculate the scale of the photograph and state by the Representative Fraction.

The Cotswolds

Question paper 1—Map 4

1. (a) State the distance in kilometres by road, and the direction, between Stanway church (061323) and Broadway church (095373).
   (b) Identify the O.S. symbols given at the following grid references: 048325; 075383; 118383; 096337; 114336; 016324; and between 063353 and 056339.
   (c) Calculate the average gradient of the track leading from the Fort at 081335 to Stanton Village at 067341.
2. Describe the course of the A44 road from the eastern edge of the map to Broadway continuing south by the A46.
3. Describe in detail the course of the main north—south railway.
4. Describe the distribution of orchards on the map and suggest reasons for their situation.

Question paper 2—Map 4

1. (a) Reduce the map-extract to half-scale, as outlined in Chapter 2, and insert the following:
   (i) 76-metre contour line: (ii) river Isbourne.
   Add short linear scale, the Representative Fraction and an orientation sign.
   The map falls into three physical regions—the dissected upland, the lowland and an isolated knoll.
   (b) Print boldly on the map, in appropriate places, the following terms: back or dip slope; scarp face; outlier; vale; one example of a dry valley; and by a dotted line insert and name the watershed.
2. Draw a cross-section from 005350 to 125322, and by symbols indicate the nature of the rocks; mark by arrows and name where the section crosses a major river; a footpath; a major road; a tributary; a main railway line and an area of mixed woodland.
3. (a) Describe the site and situation of Broadway.
   (b) Suggest reasons for its growth as the largest settlement on the map.

Supplementary questions—Map 4

1. Cover the map with tracing paper and mark off the river Isbourne, all the minor streams and other water features, e.g. ponds, lakes, moats. Is there any evidence suggesting how the upland farms obtain their water supplies?
2. Describe the physical features crossed on a walk from Laverton, via Shenbarrow Hill to Stanway, using footpaths and trackways only.
3. Explain in detail why a tunnel was constructed on the railway line in grid square 0130.
4. Determine by construction of a cross-section whether the church near the railway line at Gretton (005305) can be seen from the top of Oat Hill (096335).

North Downs, Hollingbourne

Question paper 1 — Map 5

1. Explain the meaning of the following: BS (8354); A (8254); 144 (8359); W (8458); BICKNOR CP.
2. Calculate to the nearest square kilometre the area of woodland shown on the map.
3. From the sketch-map (see Fig. 36), trace off the outline of a third-order system of valleys. Draw in the perimeter of the catchment basin and show the orders of the valley segments.
4. List the map evidence which indicates that there are problems of water supply in this area.

Question paper 2 — Map 5

1. Describe in detail the features of the railway shown on the map.
2. Draw a sketch-section of the map taken diagonally from the south-west to the north-east corner. Annotate the section to show physical features.
3. Calculate the average gradient of the road from Broad Street (830567) to spot height 188 (835573).
4. Prepare a map on tracing paper showing the distribution of farms. (Indicate each farmhouse by means of a dot or cross.) Comment on the *density* of farms, and on the *pattern* of distribution.

Supplementary questions — Map 5

1. Where were the pilgrims going along the Pilgrim's Way?
2. Draw a sketch-section through the village of Hollingbourne from south-west to north-east, and add to it a line representing the water-table. Give reasons from map evidence for the position of the line you have drawn.
3. What might the rock have been used for that was quarried in grid square 8455?
4. Prepare a small guide book to the map area showing by text, explanatory maps and diagrams, those features likely to interest the tourist.
5. Attempt to discover the meaning of Deneholes (8656). Explain why they are found in this part of the North Downs. (You may need to consult a book on archaeology.)

Ingleborough

Question paper 1 — Map 6

1. On the B6255 from Ingleton there are six milestones shown on the map. Calculate by means of the R.F. how many kilometre stones would be required to replace them.
2. Draw a sketch-section west to east across the map through Ingleborough Hill, and mark on it: limestone outcrops; river gorge; rough grazing.
3. Describe the features you would see on a journey from Thornton in Lonsdale (685736) along the road to the northern edge of the map.
4. Explain why this area is attractive to tourists.

Question paper 2 — Map 6

1. Suggest a reason for the steep gradients shown on the minor roads entering Ingleton from the north-east.
2. Determine whether it is possible to see Dale House (722757) from the summit of Ingleborough.
3. Use both Maps 5 and 6 to explain in detail how rain falling within grid square 7574 reaches Clapham Beck in square 7570.
4. What features would you expect to see below ground at Braithwaite Wife Hole (743762).

Supplementary questions — Map 6

1. Suggest the use of the Shooting Boxes shown on the map.
2. This part of northern England lay in the path of former glaciers and ice sheets. Give any map evidence that might indicate the effects of ice action.
3. List, by means of grid references, examples of the following: rock outcrop of horizontal strata; rocks of the Coal Measures; a dry gorge; mineral line.
4. Describe and explain the distribution of woodland over the map.
5. If you were obliged to descend Ingleborough Hill from the summit on a pitch-black night in order to reach the main road that runs to Ingleton what precautions would you take to ensure selecting a safe route?
6. What are the physical features depicted on Maps 5 and 6 that identify the landscape as karst?
7. Contrast the valleys drained by the rivers Doe and Ribble.

The Cairngorms

Question paper 1 — Map 7

1. Assume that you are standing on the summit of Cairngorm and facing due south. List, by means of grid references (and names where given), all the corries to be seen as you move in a clockwise direction through 360°.
2. On an enlarged sketch-map, contained by grid lines—eastings 94 to 97 and northings 97 to 00—illustrate and name the features of highland glaciation. (Compare Fig. 21b).
3. What is the average gradient of the footpath along Strath Nethy from the northern edge of the map to The Saddle?
4. Construct: (a) an annotated cross-section from Cairngorm summit to Beinn Mheadhoin to show the main features of Loch Avon and its valley; (b) a sketch-section through the middle of the lake to show the underwater features. Using both sections, comment on the origin of Loch Avon.

Question paper 2 — Map 7

1. List, by means of named examples and grid references, the following features of highland glaciation: hanging valley; hanging waterfall; truncated spur; arête; vertical rock cliff; intersecting corries; scree.
2. Describe the physical features to be seen along the footpath through the Lairig Ghru.
3. Prepare a tracing of the catchment basin of the river system flowing into the western end of Loch Avon. Number the stream channels and determine the order number of the catchment. See Figs. 20a and 20b.
4. Why are the ski-tows and chair-lifts on the northern slopes of Cairngorm and not elsewhere on the map?

Supplementary questions — Map 7

1. Take the tracing of the catchment prepared for question 3 above, and prepare a table of stream measurements as shown in Figs. 20a and 20b. Calculate the bifurcation ratio and the drainage density of the catchment.
2. Suggest, with reasons, the nature of the forested area in the north of the map.
3. Carefully examine the drainage systems over the entire map and attempt to demonstrate how highland glaciation has altered the pre-glacial drainage pattern.
4. Suggest ways in which the area might be further developed for the tourist.
5. Plate 4 shows part of the map area in winter. Loch Avon is visible in the south-east corner of the photograph with the summit of Cairngorm and Strath Nethy also identifiable north of the loch.
   (a) What is the scale of the photograph?
   (b) Use both Map 7 and the photograph to comment on the distribution of snow in relation to the major physical features.

Fort William

Question paper 1 — Map 8

1. Explain the meaning of the following O.S. symbols: P (125728); LC (097767); CH (137762); P (096745).
2. Show how the course followed by the A82(T) across the map is related to the physical geography of the area.
3. Draw sketch-maps: (a) to show the site, and (b) to show the situation of Fort William.
4. Explain in detail the advantages of the site near Corpach for the Pulp and Paper Mills. Illustrate the answer with a sketch-map.

Question paper 2 — Map 8

1. Describe the view seen by a passenger on a boat travelling north-east along Loch Linnhe towards the pier at Fort William.
2. How long would it take a climber to reach the summit of Ben Nevis, from the Achintee Hotel, keeping to a recognised footpath and maintaining an average speed of 6 kilometres per hour? The climber should take the longer of the two routes marked on the map.
3. Describe the course of the Caledonian Canal and demonstrate how it overcomes problems of relief.
4. Draw an enlarged sketch-map of the Aluminium Works and the Carbon Works and annotate it to show transport facilities and electricity supply.

Supplementary questions — Map 8

1. Identify one area of marked radial drainage.
2. Describe and attempt to explain the physical features around Stronchreggan—0772.
3. If you were commissioned to build a small marina for pleasure boats where would you locate it—and why?
4. Study the photograph, Plate 5, and check the accuracy of the corresponding part of the map. List any differences between the map and photograph.
5. Plan a 'round trip' from the Pony Trekking Centre for a day's ride, keeping mainly to the open countryside.
6. If winter snows lie in this area from January to May down to the 300-metre contour how would they affect the economic activity of the area?

Alloa

Question paper 1—Map 9

1. (a) Draw a sketch-map of the area shown and divide into physical regions. Add appropriate physical names to each region.
   (b) Compare the physical features of the valleys of the rivers Devon and Forth.
2. Find good examples of each of the following, quoting grid references in each case: Ox-bow Lake; Sand Bank; Rock Outcrop; Viaduct; Club House; Spoil Heap.
3. Describe the course taken by the old railway from 867900 through Alloa to the station at Dollar.
4. Produce a sketch-map to illustrate concisely the site of Alloa.

Question paper 2—Map 9

1. State: (a) the direction of Myreton Hill (858980), from New Sauchie church (897945);
   (b) the shortest distance by: (i) road, (ii) rail from the main line station in Alloa to the station at Dollar.
2. Relate the distribution of woodland shown on the map to both elevation and relief.
3. Calculate the gradient of the small stream in grid square 8797, terminating at the secondary road near the Golf Course.
4. Describe the site and the situation of Dollar, and account for its growth.

Supplementary questions—Map 9

1. Explain the origin of the Inches in the course of the river Forth.
2. Find examples of:
   (i) parish boundaries,
   (ii) county and parish boundaries,
   (iii) electricity transmission lines,
   (iv) Scottish National Trust properties,
   (v) ancient monuments.
   Locate each example by grid reference.
3. What stage of river development is shown by the part of the river Devon that appears on the map? Give reasons for your answer.
4. Examine closely the distribution of small mineral working lines and railway lines in relation to the most likely industrial development in the region.
5. Locate the area shown on the photograph, Plate, 1, and name the settlements shown.
6. Give four-figure grid references for the following:
   (i) the factory block in the foreground,
   (ii) the triangular-shaped housing estate to the extreme right in the middle distance,
   (iii) a railway engine in full steam,
   (iv) the isolated farm in the left middle distance.
7. State the differences between the valley of the river Devon and the Silver Glen.
8. Explain how the photograph supplements map information about land use in this area.

Warwick and Leamington

Question paper 1—Map 10

1. On a map, drawn to a scale of 1:50,000, mark and name all the water features. Attempt to explain why a canal has been built across this area.
2. Describe the view you would have looking south from the tower of Warwick Castle.
3. Describe, in relation to the relief, the 'old core' of Warwick (see also Fig. 42a).
4. Contrast the urban morphology, i.e. the layout of buildings, of the central parts of Warwick and Leamington.

Question paper 2—Map 10

1. Prepare a direct tracing from the map to show the built areas of Warwick and Leamington. Indicate by appropriate shading the following categories of buildings: medieval; Georgian; Victorian; industrial. Compare with Figs. 42a and 42b.
2. Compare the sites of Warwick and Leamington.
3. Comment on the location of: (a) the Race Course, (b) the Sewage Works, at Warwick.
4. If you were setting up a small firm manufacturing furniture in this area and had unrestricted choice, where would you locate. Give reasons for your choice.

Supplementary questions—Map 10

1. What is the meaning of letter (a) in grid square 2966?
2. What is the orientation of the photograph, Plate 6?
3. Examine together the topographic map and Fig. 42b. Suggest reasons for the designation of conservation areas as shown in Fig. 42b.
4. Describe the pattern of houses to the north of the main road in the suburb of Milverton.
5. Prepare a sketch-map showing all the main roads on the map extract. Indicate two routes for a person living near the school at Whitnash (3263) and travelling to work in The Cape (2765). Which route is likely to be the quicker during the busiest times of the day?
6. Suggest the reasons for the growth of industry in grid square 2765.
7. If you were the Chief Planner for Warwick and Leamington where would you locate: (a) new sites for industry; (b) new housing estates? Give reasons for your choice of locations.
8. What is the map evidence that suggests that this area is attractive to tourists?

Chapter nine River valleys and coastal features:
A: Pershore (Map 1)
B: Tenby (Map 2 and Plate 2)

Both maps are published by the Ordnance Survey in their 1:25,000 Second Series. The Tenby map of part of the Pembrokeshire coast of South Wales shows fine cliff and shore features, but also river and valley features inland of the coast. The Pershore map shows a section of the middle course of the river Avon downstream from Evesham in the new county of Hereford and Worcester before the river eventually joins the Severn at Tewkesbury. On both maps the contours are drawn at 5-metre intervals supplemented by spot heights given to the nearest metre.

A: Pershore (Map 1)

Relief

The area is one of gentle relief through which the river Avon flows in a broad valley, up to 2 kilometres wide in places, between low hills and ridges. By the water's edge the bank at its lowest point is 12 metres above sea-level, and the highest point on the map is the summit of Allesborough Hill (939466) 56 metres, giving a range of relief of 44 metres. A close study of the contours and the sketch-map, Fig. 31, shows that the valley is asymmetrical in cross-section, and that this asymmetry alternates downriver. It is caused by the undercutting of the river on the outer bank of the meander, producing a river cliff with a gentle slip-off slope on the inner side of the meander. As the river continues to cut down as well as sideways it has left part of its former plain as a broad and flat river terrace. In the north of the map this lies between 20 and 25 metres, and in the middle and south between 15 and 20 metres above sea-level. The upland is gently undulating and only two small brooks have cut small subsidiary valleys through it.

Drainage

The flood plain is easily recognised by the river banks where it is split up into large fields and crossed in places (9443 and 9442) by drainage ditches. In the north the river is embanked. This might be a natural levee, although certain sections are straight and suggest they have been strengthened by man. Near Cherry Orchard Barn (957464) the embankment heads well away from the river and might indicate a former course. Only a short distance further downstream near Pershore the Avon has clearly been straightened at the Weir. At 930424 the river takes an acute bend, known here as Swan's Neck, and it looks likely that at high flood the river would cut through the 'neck' and create an ox-bow lake. The many weirs on the river may mark 'breaks of slope' in the long profile where natural braiding has occurred with small islands or 'aits' in midstream. Man has stretched dams between these islands and the banks and these raise water levels. This provides greater depths for navigation, but locks are required to lift and lower boats over the weirs and the increase in water depth is also used to drive mill-wheels—the buildings set astride the channels at 952454 and 956468 are likely to be water-mills.

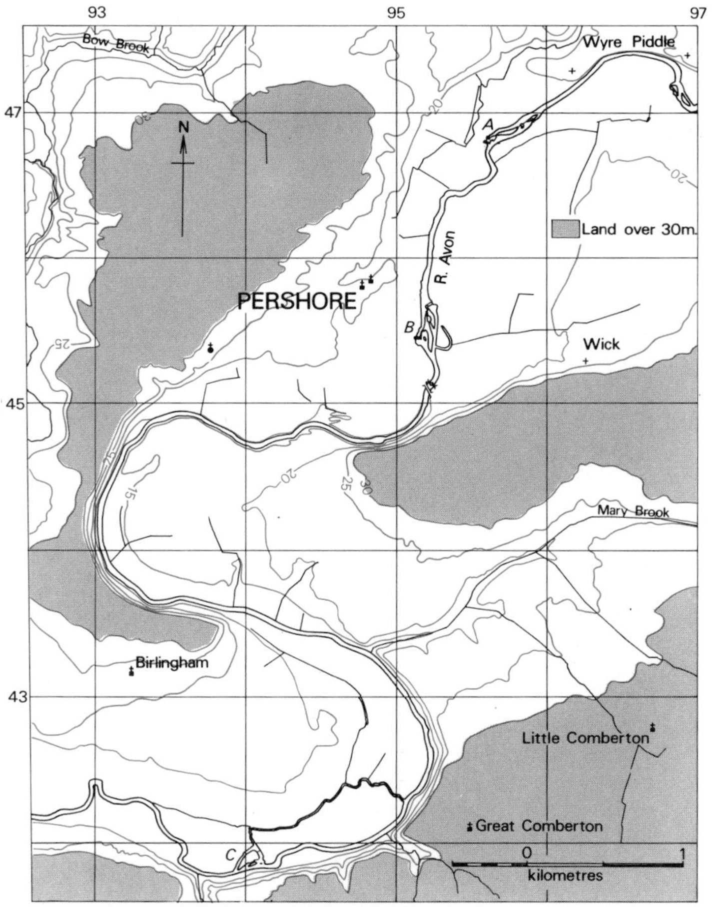

Fig. 31 Sketch-map of the Pershore map.

Settlement

Pershore is the main settlement and only town. The small nucleated villages of Great and Little Comberton, and Birlingham, are located on the upland, and other villages have established themselves on the edge of the flood plain at dry-point sites (cf. fen-edge villages, Fig. 24b) at Wick and Pensham. Nafford is only a hamlet located at a footbridge crossing of the river.

Pershore: Site and situation

The site occupies about 1.5 square kilometres on ground rising between 16 and 30 metres above the river on its west bank. The oldest part of the town seems to be along the A44 closest to the river where building is dense and narrow gardens behind the buildings run down to the waterfront. Close by the town centre is a spacious park: modern housing estates have been built to the west and north of the town.

The situation is that of a water-shunning settlement on the low valley side-slopes of the Avon where a main route from the east could cross the river and link up with other main roads on the western bank, marked by both the modern and medieval bridges.

Apart from the villages and hamlets the rest of the settlement is seen in the distribution of farms which reach a moderate density across the map, except within the flood plain.

Sketch-maps illustrating the site and situation of Pershore and Tenby are included as Figs. 33 and 34.

Communications

Three sets of lock gates (A, B, C on Fig. 31) along the river Avon suggest some water craft, but the river is too narrow and bends too much to be of great importance for commercial traffic. This is confirmed by an absence of landing quays and jetties anywhere along the river's course, even at Pershore, and no signs of a continuous towing path by the riverside.

There is no railway shown on the map nor any evidence of an airfield. All significant communication, therefore, must be by road. The terrain presents no serious difficulty to road construction and the major control over routes is Pershore bridge, controlling traffic across the river.

Land use

The obvious use of land is for agriculture, particularly for orchard fruits. In addition to the O.S. 'orchard' symbol the name is incorporated in three place names: Orchard Farm, Hands Orchard and Cherry Orchard Barn; moreover at Avonbank (957438) there is the Pershore Institute of Horticulture. Note the incidence of glasshouses at many farms. Apart from farming, the Tyddesley Wood and the nearby Rifle Range represent another form of land use, but there is no other direct evidence of development other than such named buildings as schools, police stations and sewage works.

Summary

This is a lowland landscape produced mainly by the work of the river that flows through it. The slopes above the flood plain are declining and gentle in gradient except at the river cliffs. The physical elements of the landscape have, in no way, prevented Man's occupance and the cultural features show that he has made good use of it.

B: Tenby (Map 2 and Plate 2)

Study the map extract together with the sketch-map which shows the significant elements of both the physical and cultural characteristics of the area. Note that the alternative name for Tenby is given in the Welsh language, but unlike the Cairngorm map where most of the place names are in the original Gaelic, on the Tenby sheet almost all the names seem to have an English derivation. The photograph of the north part of the town and Castle Hill, (Plate 2), should be examined with reference to the equivalent part of the map. As the photograph covers only a small part of the map the detail is extremely good. The aircraft must have flown obliquely across the town to obtain the three-dimensional effect, for not only is the street pattern shown with great clarity, but also the small houses and gardens and parked vehicles. With a hand lens it is even possible to distinguish the makes of motor cars.

Relief and drainage

The map shows a deeply dissected plateau reaching the sea in rugged cliffs except where the Knightson Brook and its tributary (unnamed), enter the sea in a broad, sandy estuary. The flat summits reach just over 90 metres in the north and decline slightly to the south. The incised valleys are narrow and the sides steep, but rise to rounded shoulders separated by smooth spurs giving a generally rolling appearance of open upland swells and wooded valley floors.

The small Knightson Brook enters the sea (the Bristol Channel) in a meandering course across a broad marshy flat before reaching the north end of a sandy bay (129004). It must be presumed that the water reaches the sea under the beach deposits as there is no evidence of a river mouth. To the north of Tenby a series of small streams flow seawards in steep little valleys and tumble in small waterfalls over the cliffs to the beaches below. The upland is characterised by a large number of springs marking the risings of tributary streams. This suggests a high water-table with a dry summit area.

Coastal features

The coastline shows cliffing along almost its entire length. North of the Tenby promontory there is a succession of small bays alternating with rocky headlands; cliffs rise from sea level over 70 metres in many places. Even in the south where The Burrows and South

Beach exhibit an estuarine bay, the opposing headlands are also cliffed. Note the position of Mean High Water—everywhere at the base of the cliffs indicating that the sea is actually eroding the coastline at the present time. The presence of coastal waterfalls also confirms this view, the former middle and lower parts of the valleys having disappeared into the sea.

The origin of the bay between Penally and Tenby can now be considered. The shape of the lower valley here is like that of a drowned estuary or ria—steep but rounded side slopes with a broad valley floor. But the outfall has been blocked by sand drifted by waves across the bay, and this, in turn, has caused deposition by the river and the creation of alluvial marshes. The present sand accumulation appears confined to the South Beach and the older beach deposits, now inland and beyond the limit of normal high tides, have been reworked by the wind into dunes and converted by man to a golf links.

Settlement

Tenby is the chief settlement: a seaside town built around a rocky promontory with the advantage of two fine beaches (see Plate 2). The core of the town seems to be above the North Beach and the remains of an old castle may represent the site of earliest settlement. Note also the fort on St Catherine's Island in a superb position for coastal observation.

The only other settlement of any size is the street village of Penally, on rising ground across the bay south-west from Tenby. Elsewhere the settlements are no more than hamlets at Broadfield (131037) and Twy Cross (128033), and several scattered farms.

Site and situation

If we are correct in deducing that the earliest site was above the North Beach and around the Castle Hill peninsula the town has spread both northwards and inland, and towards the South Beach and The Marshes. The site remains elevated between 10 and 20 metres above sea-level near the sea, but has occupied rising ground up to 60 metres in Upper Hill Park and Lady Park. It is very clear from the map, by the ground plan of the buildings, that the highest areas are those of most recent development. The old core was located on the cliff top above Mean High Water, but the site is also constrained by the marshes of the former estuary to the west. The significance of this control is read in place-name evidence: Saltern, The Marshes, Marsh Farm, Holloway Bridge, etc.

The main headland at Tenby is densely settled both with public and private buildings. There is little open space on this older site but later development has allowed for parks and playing fields.

Figure 34 illustrates the situation of Tenby. Remember that the situation of a place is the relationship of its site to the surrounding land and water features, i.e. its geographical setting.

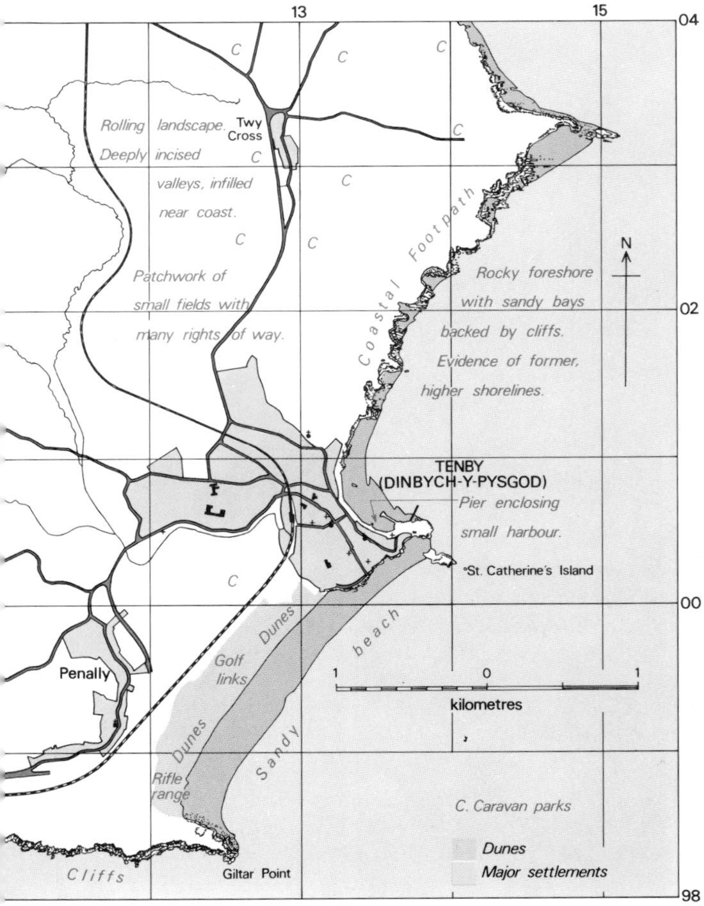

Fig. 32 Sketch-map of the Tenby map.

PLATE 2 Tenby

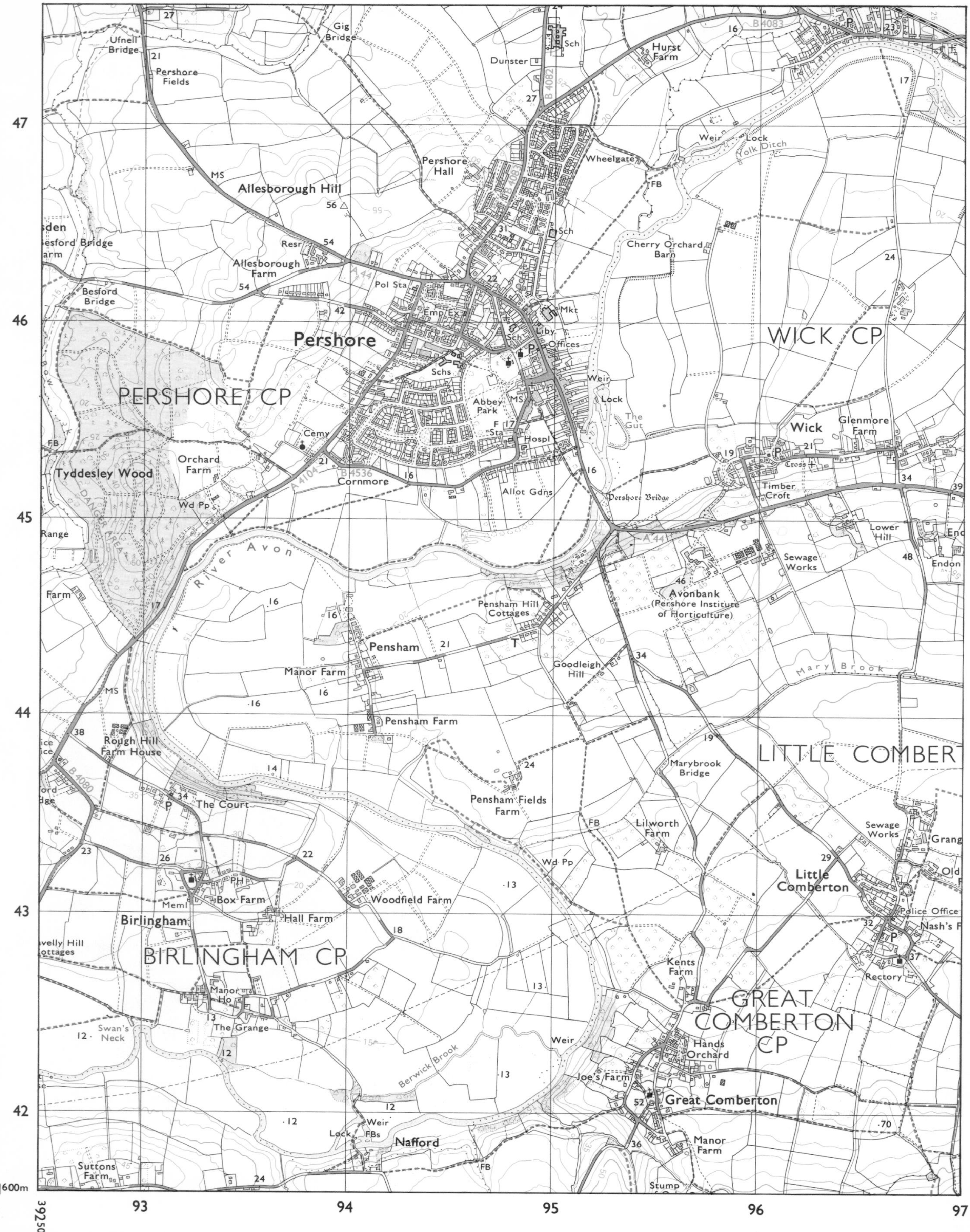
Pershore
PERSHORE CP
WICK CP
LITTLE COMBERT
BIRLINGHAM CP
GREAT COMBERTON CP
Gig Bridge
Ufnell Bridge
Pershore Fields
Dunster
Sch
Hurst Farm
B 4083
B 4082
Pershore Hall
Allesborough Hill
MS
Wheelgate
Weir
Lock
Yolk Ditch
FB
Cherry Orchard Barn
Besford Bridge
Resr
Allesborough Farm
Pol Sta
Emp Ex
Mkt
Liby
Offices
Schs
Abbey Park
F Sta
Hospl
Cemy
The Gut
Wick
Glenmore Farm
Cross
Timber Croft
Tyddesley Wood
Orchard Farm
Wd Pp
Cornmore
Allot Gdns
Pershore Bridge
B 4536
A 4104
A 44
Range
Lower Hill
Endon
River Avon
Sewage Works
Avonbank
(Pershore Institute of Horticulture)
Pensham Hill Cottages
Pensham
Manor Farm
Goodleigh Hill
Mary Brook
Pensham Farm
Rough Hill Farm House
B 4080
The Court
Marybrook Bridge
Pensham Fields Farm
Lilworth Farm
Grange
Box Farm
Meml
PH
Woodfield Farm
Hall Farm
Birlingham
Little Comberton
Police Office
Nash's F
Rectory
Kents Farm
Manor Ho
The Grange
Swan's Neck
Hands Orchard
Joe's Farm
Berwick Brook
Great Comberton
Weir
Lock
FBs
Nafford
Manor Farm
Suttons Farm
Stump
24|600m
392500m
93
94
95
96
97
47
46
45
44
43
42

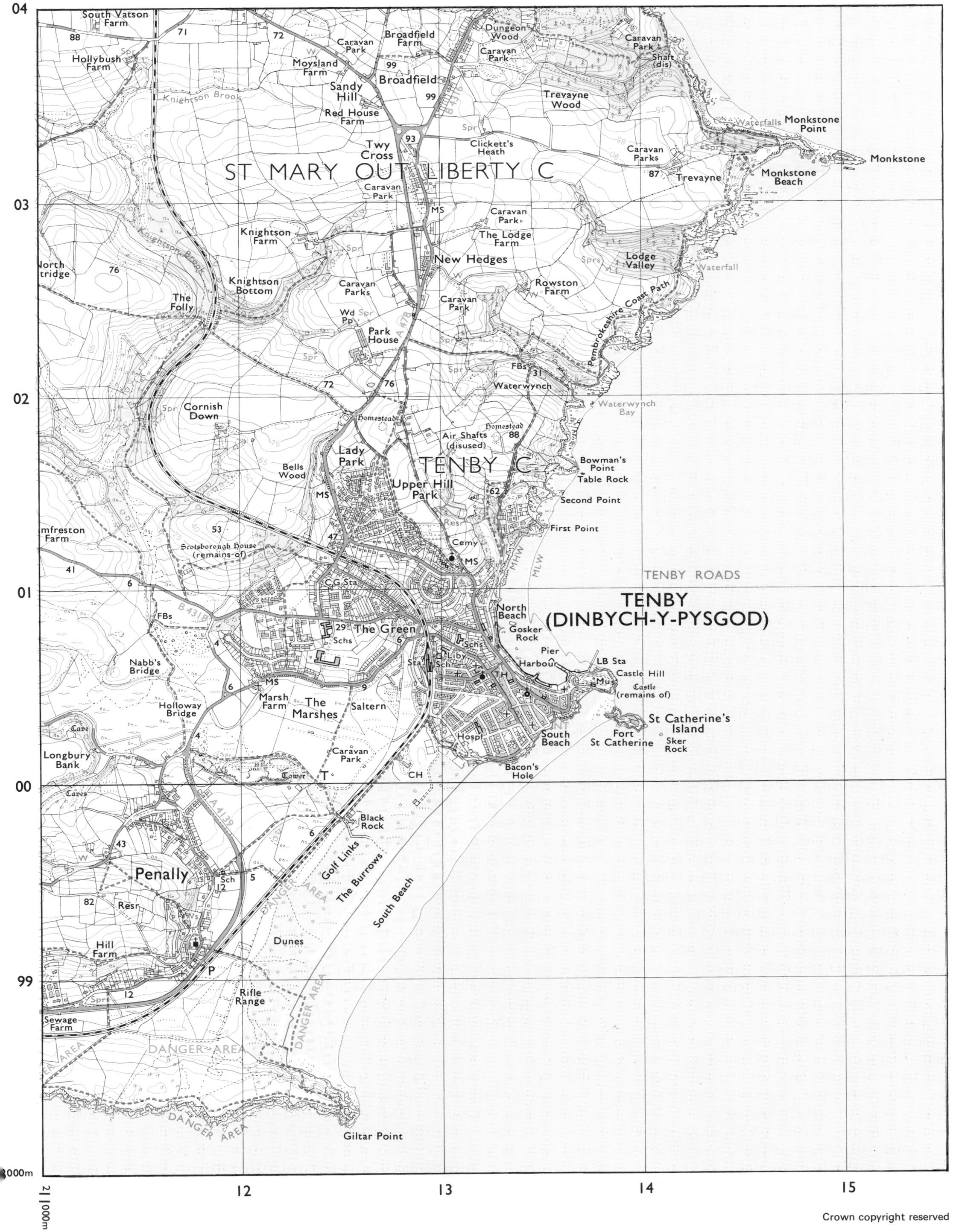
South Vatson Farm
Hollybush Farm
Knightson Brook
Caravan Park
Broadfield Farm
Moysland Farm
Sandy Hill
Broadfield
Dungeon Wood
Trevayne Wood
Red House Farm
Twy Cross
Clickett's Heath
Waterfalls
Monkstone Point
Monkstone
Caravan Parks
Trevayne
Monkstone Beach
ST MARY OUT LIBERTY C
Knightson Farm
The Lodge Farm
New Hedges
North Stridge
Knightson Bottom
The Folly
Rowston Farm
Lodge Valley
Waterfall
Pembrokeshire Coast Path
Park House
Waterwynch
Waterwynch Bay
Cornish Down
Homestead
Air Shafts (disused)
Lady Park
TENBY C
Bells Wood
Upper Hill Park
Bowman's Point
Table Rock
Second Point
First Point
Scotsborough House (remains of)
Cemy
MHW
MLW
TENBY ROADS
C G Sta
The Green
North Beach
Gosker Rock
TENBY
(DINBYCH-Y-PYSGOD)
Pier
Harbour
LB Sta
Castle Hill
Mus
Castle (remains of)
Nabb's Bridge
Holloway Bridge
Marsh Farm
The Marshes
Saltern
St Catherine's Island
Fort St Catherine
Sker Rock
South Beach
Hospl
Bacon's Hole
Longbury Bank
Caravan Park
Tower
Black Rock
Penally
Golf Links
The Burrows
South Beach
Resr
Dunes
Hill Farm
Rifle Range
Sewage Farm
DANGER AREA
Giltar Point
04
03
02
01
00
99
12
13
14
15

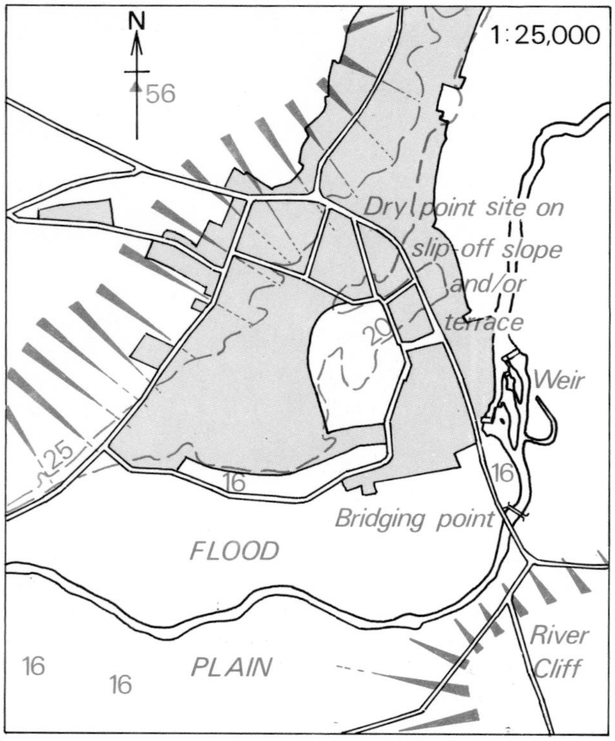

Fig. 33 Sketch-map to show the site of Pershore.

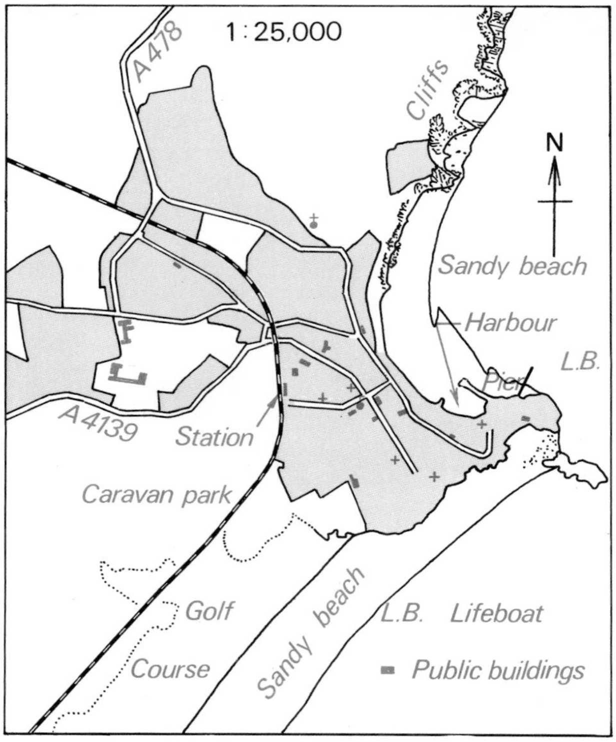

Fig. 34 Sketch-map to show the situation and functions of Tenby.

Communications

Note how the pattern of road communication differs markedly from that made by the railway. The main roads avoid the principal valley and follow the plateau summit from the north to converge on Tenby. On the A478 at Twy Cross a new section of road has foreshortened the route and bypassed the settlement. Similarly in the south the A4139 has been routed away from the village of Penally.

On the other hand the railway line makes use of the Knightson Brook into Tenby from the north, negotiating the middle hill-slopes by means of cuttings, and entering the station over a viaduct (see Plate 2). The line then swings to the south-west across the marshes and dunes on a straight course without providing any obvious service for the people of Penally. We should expect on a coastal map some evidence of communication by sea—note the Harbour at Tenby and the Lifeboat Station.

Summary

The physical processes that are mainly responsible for the principal elements of this landscape are streams and waves. The resistant rocks form a plateau inland that is deeply dissected into small valleys which either lead towards the main bay in the south, or have been truncated by marine erosion to form steep cliffed sections in the north. A relatively recent rise of sea-level is indicated by active wave attack at the base of the cliffs and by the dissection of the promontories into small islands. Nowhere is there any evidence of glaciation, but the effect of wind in creating sand dunes can be seen in The Burrows.

Chapter ten Fenland: The Middle Level (Map 3 and Plate 3)

The map extract shows a very typical piece of the English Fens and a small portion of the bordering upland. One of the four major rivers of the Fens, the Great Ouse, and several main drains appear on the map.

Relief

The upland area in the east, although small, is clearly a separate region and could well be divided from the rest of the map by the 15-metre contour line or the railway line could conveniently be used. The rest of the map is a well-drained lowland and heights nowhere exceed 15 metres; indeed, very careful examination shows several spot heights only just above sea-level— at 544069 and at 555053 the land is actually at sea-level.

Drainage

Of all the water-courses on the map only that of the river Ouse appears natural, winding between the embankments that show little straightening by Man. The other water-courses clearly show Man's influence either in part, or along the entire straight course of the drains. Several types of drain are shown:

(i) field drains that are, in fact, ditches around individual fields;

(ii) larger connecting drains, e.g. Common Lode into which the field drains flow; and

(iii) the main level drains, e.g. the section of the Middle Level Main Drain.

All the main drains are embanked, indicating a high water level. Careful examination of the map will reveal spot heights at or near sea-level very close to these drains and this suggests that the river level is above that of the surrounding fields. At Denver, 587010, several important features of the drainage should be noted: the two major drains joining the Ouse above the Sluice Gate on the river; the controlling locks on the western drain; and to the east of the river a drain unconnected to the main system running parallel to the river carrying seaward water from the upland.

Settlement

The principal settlements are the villages and one small town, Downham Market.

The villages

Villages are indicated on the 1:50,000 map by the Ordnance Survey use of a characteristic style of printing as seen in the name 'Outwell' (5104). At Outwell and Three Holes we see typical street-type villages, the buildings strung out along both sides of the road. This settlement plan is seen along the two main roads entering Outwell from the south-west and south-east. On a smaller scale, Nordelph shows this form. Away from these villages buildings follow the roads and droves as in the 'ribbon development' along Barroway Drove.

The other villages in the east are along a marked natural line from Denver through Wimbotsham to Stow Bardolph. This line marks the edge of the drained lowland and coincides approximately with the 15-metre contour. There is some evidence to suggest a spring line at this height as tiny streams emerge near the villages and flow to join the Ouse. Each village is nucleated around a crossroads and is linked by the trunk road, the A10, which seeks to avoid the upland and wetter lowlands.

Downham Market

This small town is also situated on the same natural line, but has outgrown its neighbours. The map does not suggest clearly the causes of this growth except that it is a focus of main roads, but the railway station is outside the town and the river Ouse 1.4 kilometres due west shows no sign of a river port.

Dispersed settlements

The absence of large parkland estates so familiar in other parts of Britain could indicate both the recent occupation of the farmland and its high fertility. This is supported by the density of farms. The farms are evenly distributed, served by minor roads and trackways.

Land use

Woodland is entirely absent from the drained lowland and there is much evidence to confirm the impression of a very fertile soil. The high density of farm buildings and the roads serving them has been noted. The fields are small and the network of drains is such that it could only be maintained by a prosperous farming community.

As the general level of the land is close to sea-level, flooding of the fields seems likely and we might expect pasture to be the principal land use. The land around Outwell and Three Holes is under orchards and there is no evidence to indicate other forms of land use.

Industrial occupations are conspicuously absent from the map apart from the word 'Mills' near Downham Market, at 603030.

Summary

The place-name evidence of 'Fen' is sufficient by itself to fix the location of the map and the character of the lowland. With this knowledge we can turn to the supporting evidence of the drains and levels to see that this is one of the most intensively farmed areas in Britain. In fact, the drained land is mainly devoted to arable farming and market gardening. The settlements are found on small 'islands' raised slightly above fen level or along the fen edge, i.e. 'fen-line' villages.

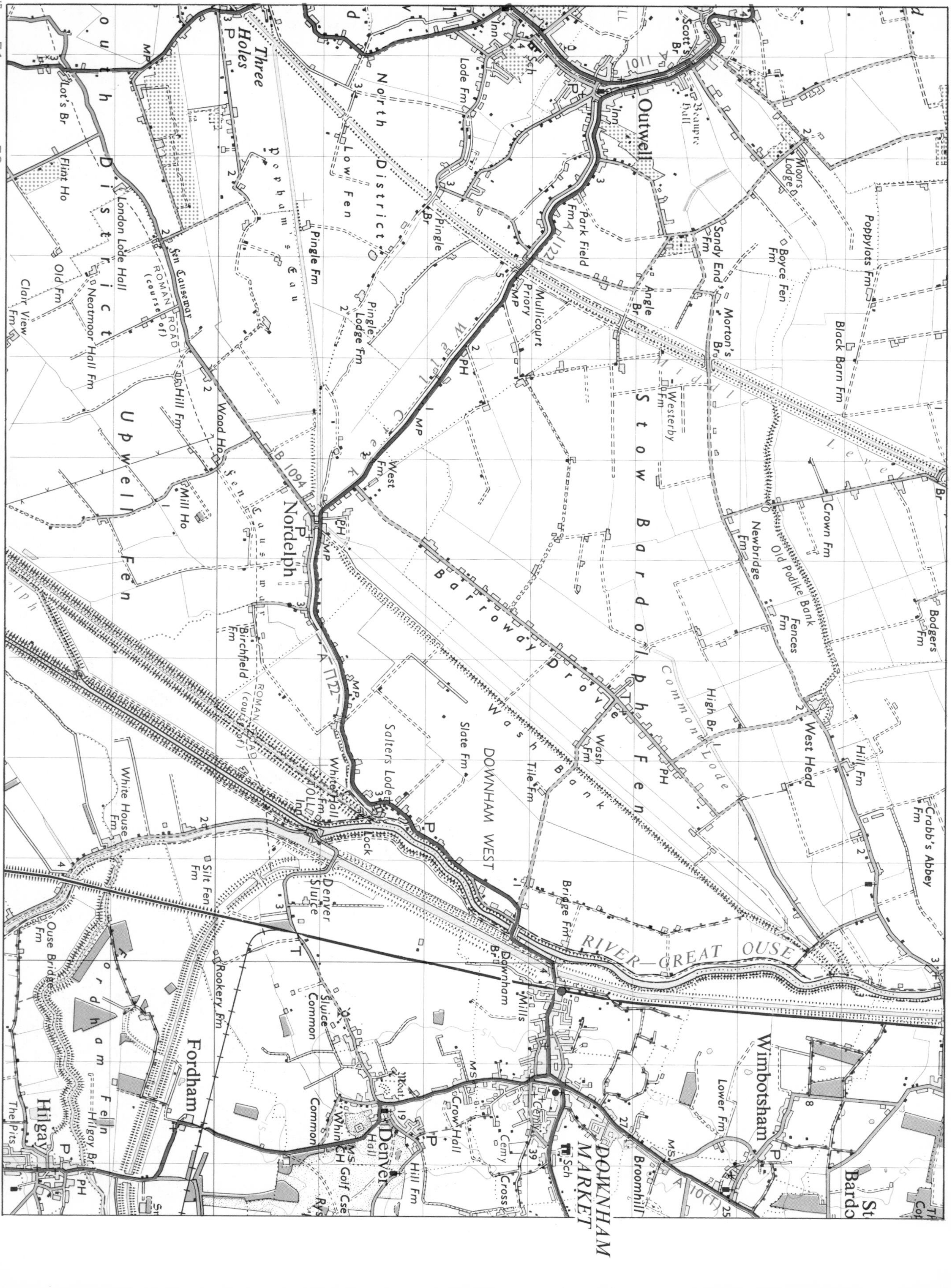
Outwell
Three Holes
North District
Low Fen
Popham's Eau
Pingle Fm
Nordelph
Upwell Fen
Stow Bardolph Fen
Barroway Drove
Wash Bank
DOWNHAM WEST
Salters Lode
Denver Sluice
RIVER GREAT OUSE
Downham Br
Sluice Common
Denver
Fordham
Hilgay
Wimbotsham
DOWNHAM MARKET
West Head
Crown Fm
Bodgers Fm
Crabb's Abbey
Boyce Fen Fm
Poppylots Fm
Black Barn Fm
Sandy End Fm
Angle Br
Morton's Br
Mullicourt Priory
Park Field Fm
West Fm
Birchfield Fm
White House Fm
Silt Fen Fm
Ouse Bridge Fm
Rookery Fm
Hill Fm
Broomhill
Lower Fm
Flint Ho
Lot's Br
Old Fm
Neatmoor Hall Fm
Wood Ho
Mill Ho
Clair View Fm
London Lode Hall
Pingle Lodge Fm
Newbridge Fm
Fences Fm
Old Podike Bank
High Br
Common Lode
Wash Fm
Slate Fm
Tile Fm
Bridge Fm
Westerby Fm
Moors Lodge
Beaupre Hall
Scott's Br
Lode Fm
Hilgay Br
The Pits
Crow Hall
Golf Cse
A 1122
B 1094
A 1011
A 10(T)

A
B
C

Chapter eleven Scarp and vale: The Cotswolds (Map 4)

The map-extract of Sheet 150 of the 1:50,000-First Series O.S. map shows part of the Cotswold scarp and the adjacent Vale of Evesham. Many of the features outlined in Chapter 4 are well represented. Examine Figs. 17a and 17b and 18a showing the origin of scarp and vale topography and then compare it with the block diagram, Fig. 35, and the map. Let us now apply our knowledge to the most significant features shown on the map.

Relief*

At the outset distinguish between Relief and Elevation. Relief here (from base of scarp slope to crest of escarpment) is roughly 200 metres, and from the lowest part of the vale to the crest the maximum relief is over 250 metres. The escarpment rises to an elevation of 319 metres, which is very high for British scarplands.

The scarp face trends approximately north-north-east to south-south-west and has been deeply dissected by small streams, producing an indented or fretted scarp. The dissection has reached an advanced stage. A small hill detached from the main escarpment exhibits a similar form to the main upland, and it appears that this knoll may have been isolated by the backward erosion of the river Isbourne and a neighbouring stream, which leaves the map south of Alderton. If this is so, the term 'outlier' should be given to the knoll.

Drainage

The uplands

The general absence of surface drainage is at once evident. The streams flowing down the scarp slope rise at approximately 200 metres, but on the back slope only one stream appears, draining south through the valley of Cutsdean (088302). Careful examination shows other valley forms indicated by the contours, e.g. the valley containing Scarborough (113309). This is a good example of a dry valley. This evidence points to a permeable rock strata. Similar waterless features are exhibited by the knoll near Dumbleton, providing further information towards confirming its origin as an outlier.

* Note that this is a First Series 1:50,000 map and that contour values are given to the nearest metre. The vertical interval, however, is 50 feet and this makes the numbering of the contours somewhat confusing.

The lowlands

With their numerous water-courses the lowlands provide a great contrast to the uplands. The major stream of the area is the river Isbourne flowing north which is joined by many tributaries on its right bank. The presence of so much surface water indicates impermeable rocks.

Settlement

The uplands

No large settlements can be found; Snowshill (0933) and Cutsdean (0830) are obviously small villages, each with a parish church. The remaining habitations are isolated farms, e.g. Peter's Farm (121363) and Toddington (0831). There is much evidence of ancient occupation of these uplands in Tumuli and Barrows (burial chambers), at (117383) and a hill-fort at (080335).

The lowlands

The settlements mainly nucleated in villages, include the following types:

(a) Scarp-foot villages, e.g. Stanway, Stanton and Buckland. Dumbleton and Broadway are situated in similar positions; the former at the base of the outlier and the latter, a street village, at the break of slope between the vale and the uplands. All these are dry sites avoiding the damp lowland where early building was possible and drinking water nearby. Note that the actual spring-line appears to be above the general height of the villages.

(b) River and stream sites, e.g. Aston Somerville, Toddington and Sedgeberrow, located within short distances from streams but slightly above the river bank.

(c) Scattered farms.

Communications

Roads and trackways

The upland area has a high density of footpaths and tracks, fenced and unfenced minor roads; the A44 road through Broadway and the B4077 are the only examples of Ministry of Transport roads Classes 1 and 2. The large number of trackways indicates a close network of communications from early times and is characteristic of the drier upland areas in Britain. The existence of so few major roads in this part of the map is probably due to the absence of large settlements and the engineering difficulties in constructing modern highways in this kind of terrain.

On the other hand, in the lowlands major roads are more in evidence with longer straight stretches and footpaths and tracks are largely missing. It is significant that the major roads here do not pass directly through the small settlements and probably link larger towns beyond the limits of the map-extract.

Railways

Two stretches of main line railway are to be seen, which avoid the greater undulations of the scarp foot, and the wetter areas of the river valleys. With the exception of a tunnel (0130) the construction of the railway appears to have presented few problems.

No other signs of communications can be found.

Land use

The widespread presence of large farms over the entire map, and orchards in the lowlands, and the absence of much rough grazing and woodland suggests that farming is the principal land use. Patches of mixed woodland are found mainly on the steeper slopes. In addition there are several large parks, probably country estates.

Only one quarry is shown (078302) and we can assume that mineral extraction is almost non-existent in this area. Nor is there any sign of industry.

Summary

We can now make some tentative conclusions, from this interpretation, about the nature of this scarpland area. The permeability of the upland is in little doubt, suggesting limestone or sandstone rocks, but confirmation of a more positive kind (e.g. named quarries, etc.) is lacking. The smooth outline of the relief and the prominent dry valleys remove the possibility of Carboniferous Limestone, and the presence of many deciduous trees and the numerous settlements suggests a richer soil than is usually found on upland sandstones. Map evidence, by itself, is not enough to prove chalk or Jurassic limestone but the student should know that chalk escarpments in Britain do not reach an elevation of more than 300 metres.

As shown in Chapter 5, the most likely rock-former of impermeable lowland is clay, but the conclusive evidence in form of clay-pits, etc. cannot be found on the map.

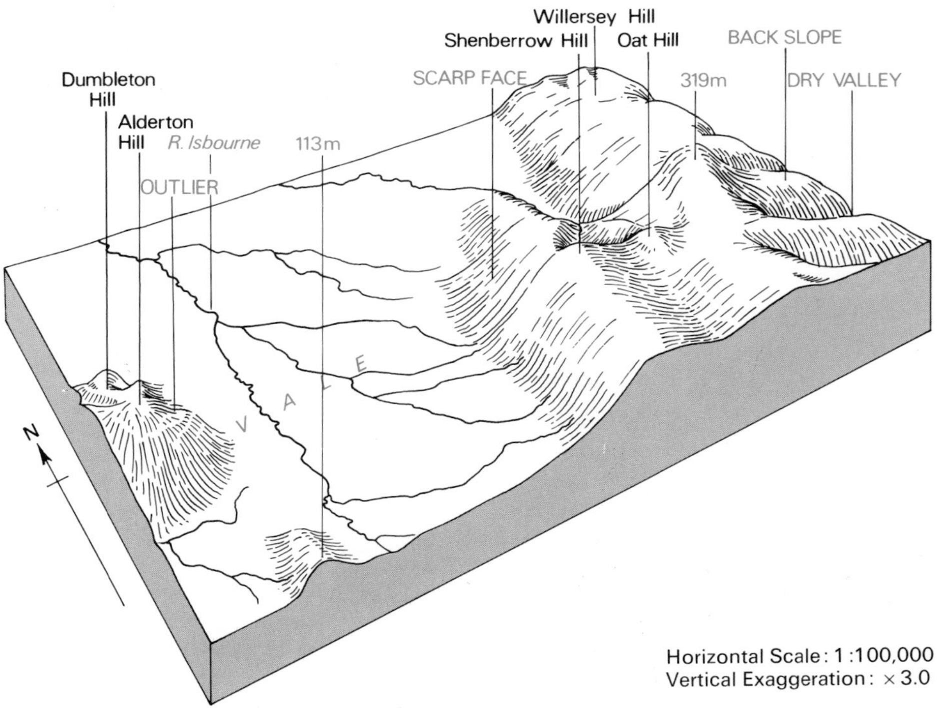

Fig. 35 Block diagram of Cotswolds map.

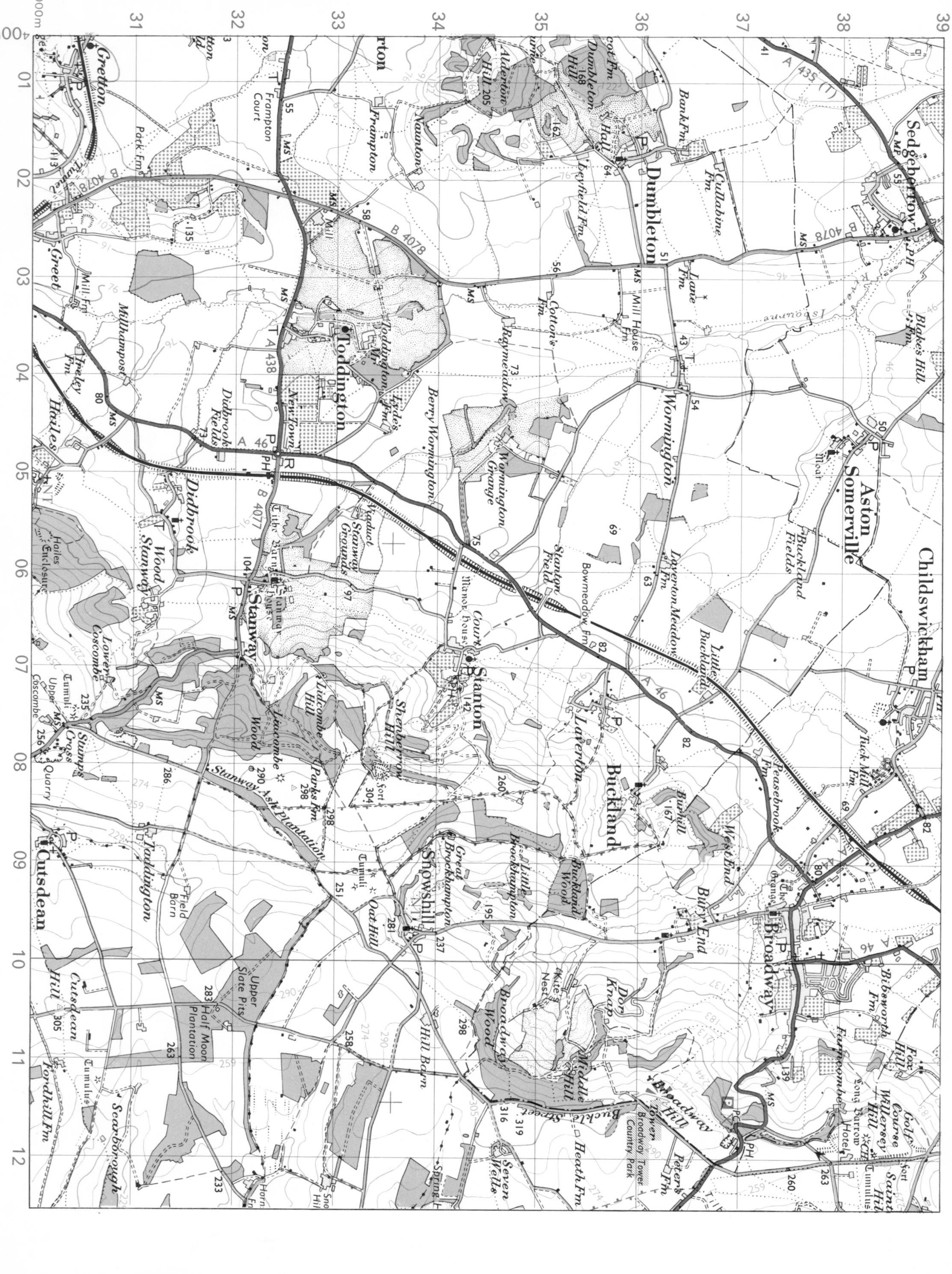
Gretton
Greet
Hailes
Didbrook
Wood Stanway
Stanway
Toddington
Dumbleton
Wormington
Aston Somerville
Childswickham
Sedgeberrow
Stanton
Laverton
Buckland
Snowshill
Broadway
Cutsdean
Broadway Hill
Broadway Tower Country Park
Dumbleton Hill
Alderton Hill
Lidcombe Hill
Shenberrow Hill
Stanway Ash Plantation
Half Moon Plantation
Upper Slate Pits
Seven Wells
Stumps Cross
Hailes Enclosure
Lower Coscombe
Upper Coscombe
Lidcombe Wood
Buckland Wood
Broadway Wood
Middle Hill
Kite's Nest
Dor Knap
Bury End
West End
Little Buckland
Laverton Meadows
Buckland Fields
Wormington Grange
Stanway Grounds
Stanton Fields
Bowmeadow Fm
Peasebrook Fm
Tuck Mill Fm
Bibsworth Fm
Farncombe
Fox Hill
Willersey Hill
Golf Course
Saintbury
Isbourne
Frampton
Frampton Court
Naunton
Berry Wormington
Didbrook Fields
Millhampost
Cotton's Fm
Raymeadow
Leyfield Fm
Cullabine Fm
Bank Fm
Lane Fm
Mill House Fm
Blakes Hill Fm
New Town
Eyde's Fm
Toddington Mr
Great Brockhampton
Little Brockhampton
Oat Hill
Hill Barn
Field Barn
Fordhill Fm
Scarborough
Cutsdean Hill
Heath Fm
Peter's Fm
Buckle Street
Stanway House
Manor House
Court
Tithe Barn
Viaduct
Quarry
Tumuli
Tumulus
Parks Fm
Park Fm
Mill Fm
Trafley Fm
Tunnel
Burhill
The Grange
Moat
Long Barrow
Hotel
Fort
A 46
A 438
A 435 (T)
B 4077
B 4078
230000m
400500m
31
32
33
34
35
36
37
38
39
01
02
03
04
05
06
07
08
09
10
11
12

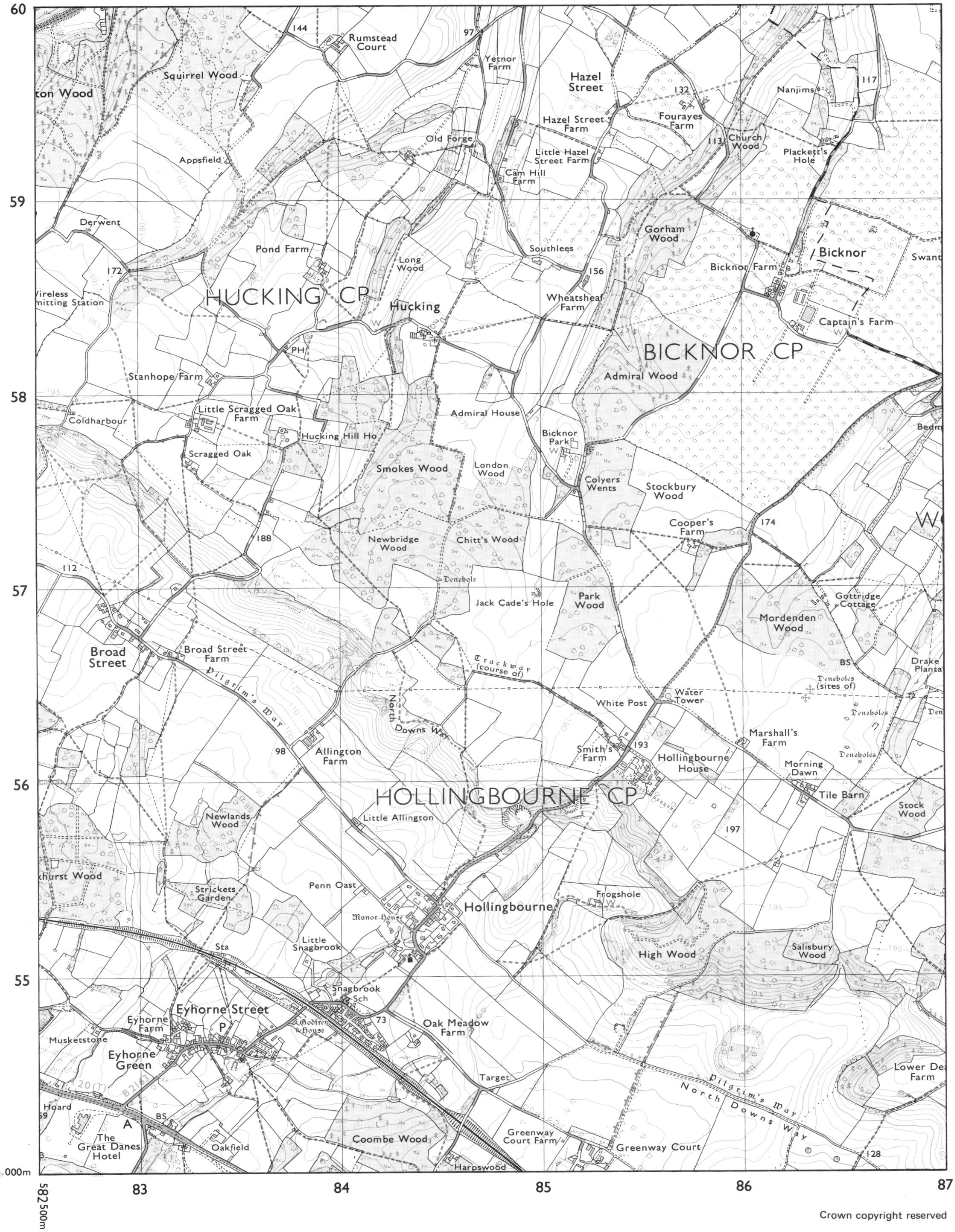
Rumstead Court
Yetnor Farm
Squirrel Wood
Hazel Street
Nanjims
Fourayes Farm
Hazel Street Farm
Old Forge
Church Wood
Plackett's Hole
Little Hazel Street Farm
Cam Hill Farm
Appsfield
Derwent
Gorham Wood
Pond Farm
Long Wood
Southlees
Bicknor
Bicknor Farm
HUCKING CP
Hucking
Wheatsheaf Farm
Captain's Farm
BICKNOR CP
Stanhope Farm
Admiral Wood
Little Scragged Oak Farm
Coldharbour
Admiral House
Hucking Hill Ho
Bicknor Park
Scragged Oak
Smokes Wood
London Wood
Colyers Wents
Stockbury Wood
Cooper's Farm
Newbridge Wood
Chitt's Wood
Jack Cade's Hole
Park Wood
Mordenden Wood
Gottridge Cottage
Broad Street
Broad Street Farm
Pilgrim's Way
Trackway (course of)
Deneholes (sites of)
Water Tower
White Post
North Downs Way
Marshall's Farm
Allington Farm
Smith's Farm
Hollingbourne House
Morning Dawn
Tile Barn
HOLLINGBOURNE CP
Stock Wood
Newlands Wood
Little Allington
Penn Oast
Strickets Garden
Frogshole
Hollingbourne
Manor House
Little Snagbrook
High Wood
Salisbury Wood
Sta
Snagbrook
Sch
Eyhorne Street
Eyhorne Farm
Godfrey House
Oak Meadow Farm
Musketstone
Eyhorne Green
Target
Pilgrim's Way
North Downs Way
Lower Farm
Hoard
The Great Danes Hotel
Oakfield
Coombe Wood
Greenway Court Farm
Greenway Court
Harpswood
83
84
85
86
87
55
56
57
58
59
60

Chapter twelve Limestone uplands:
A: North Downs, Hollingbourne (Map 5)
B: Ingleborough (Map 6)

A: North Downs, Hollingbourne (Map 5)

Reference has been made (p. 28) to those landscapes of permeable rocks where there is little surface drainage and the terrain is dissected by valleys which are, today, quite dry. Map 5 shows part of the North Downs in the county of Kent; there are a few streams in the south-west of the map flowing from the foot of an escarpment, but on the backslope the only water areas appear as ponds with no inlets and no outflow.

Relief

The most prominent relief feature is an escarpment which runs from north-west to south-east across the area (see Fig. 36). The scarp-slope rises steeply from about 130 metres to 180 metres above sea-level and the scarp face is indented and, in places, cut back to form **coombes**. Although these land forms resemble—but on a much smaller scale—the corries or cwms of glaciated highlands (see the Cairngorms, Map 7), they should clearly be distinguished from them. Corries are primarily features carved by glacier ice, whereas coombes are found predominantly in those limestone uplands of southern England that lay well beyond the furthest limits of ice advance. It is possible, however, that melting from snow patches has accentuated hollows first created by spring-sapping.

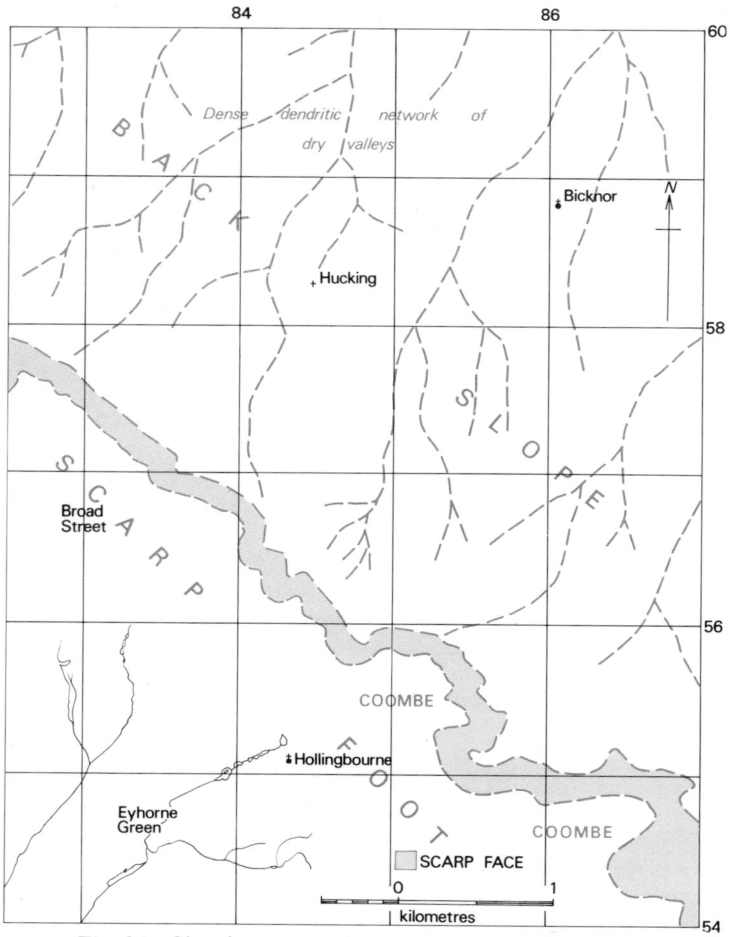

Fig. 36 Sketch-map to show physical regions of Hollingbourne map.

The back-slope is dissected by a dense network of dry valleys which have relatively steep sides, smooth floors and interlocking spurs, but rise to rounded shoulders and nearly flat summits. The whole effect is one of marked undulating relief. Note how tributary valleys join the principal valleys at smooth or **accordant** junctions precisely in the same way as a stream would join a main river.

At the foot of the scarp streams appear about the 75-metre contour and flow in a south-westerly direction. In a number of places the water is held back along the stream courses to create ponds and a small lake, possibly a reservoir, near Eyhorne Green. The streams are too small to have cut deep valleys, and occupy shallow depressions in very gently rolling lowland.

Drainage

Enough has been written already to demonstrate the marked contrast between the almost totally dry upland and the wetter lowland. The dry valleys suggest by their individual shape, and dendritic (tree-like) pattern that they have been cut by surface water when the water-table was higher than at present. This evidence is sufficient to indicate a rock of very high permeability, almost certainly a limestone.

Settlement

Settlement is small-scale and dispersed. At Hollingbourne, Eyhorne and Broad Street, villages have developed alongside the roads. On the back-slope of the upland there are only hamlets and farmsteads and almost all of these avoid the valleys. They are located on the shoulders and flatter inter-valley areas. The only case where this is not so is named characteristically Plackett's Hole (865593). The steep scarp-slope is totally devoid of any kind of habitation.

Land use

Much of the area is still wooded, mainly with deciduous trees, but there is much farming too readily identified by means of place-name evidence. In the north-east there are large orchards around the hamlet of Bicknor. As this area is part of Kent the orchards are likely to be of deciduous fruits such as apples, pears, plums and cherries. We are also reminded of another Kentish activity at Penn Oast (841555), a possible oast house used for the drying of hops. Other than these activities there is little evidence of present land use. The quarry at Hollingbourne appears to have been abandoned.

Communications

A main railway line crosses through the scarp foot zone, negotiating the low relief by means of shallow cuttings. The station at 834552 is away from the villages and approached only by footpaths. It can hardly be more than a halt. There are two ancient trackways shown, one above the scarp face, and the other, the well-known Pilgrim's Way, at the foot of the scarp. They run parallel with the escarpment avoiding the steepest slopes, but one major road and one minor do manage to overcome the gradient of the scarp-slope to link the lower with the higher ground. On the upland the road network conspicuously avoids the narrow valley floors and links the inter-valley settlements. There are very many public footpaths and a special walkers' route has been designated the North Downs Way.

Summary

There is every indication (except named evidence) that the rock forming this part of the escarpment of the North Downs is chalk. It is typically demonstrated by the undulating upland deeply dissected by valleys which are now dry. At the foot of the scarp the chalk gives way to softer rocks of a more impermeable kind and these support streams flowing from springs near the scarp foot. Nowhere is the land too elevated or exposed to prevent cultivation and the map shows evidence of long-continued occupance and land use.

The origin of dry valleys

We have established that the escarpment and back-slope are formed of chalk rock and we have noted particularly the dry valley systems that dissected the back-slope across the northern part of the map. On the next map, Ingleborough, there can be seen dry valley sections, but no complete valley systems that are streamless and, moreover, on the Ingleborough upland many streams can be traced to a point at which they disappear below ground at a sink or pot-hole. No stream sinks can be seen on the Hollingbourne map.

All those who have studied the origin of the valleys are agreed that they can only have been cut by surface water flow: the valley sides are smooth, the spurs interlock, the valley floor declines gradually to a smooth or accordant junction with a neighbouring valley. We are clearly not dealing with such processes as ice, wave or wind erosion. Some of the alternative explanations put forward for the origin of these land forms are as follows.

The pluvial theory

This assumes that at some time in the past, rainfall was much higher than now, so that the water-table rose until it cut the surface of the land, and water flowed from springs located high on the back-slope. Some valleys do have periodic flows of water even today after long spells of wet weather, but it is difficult to find evidence in the geological past when the climate was sufficiently wetter to cause a virtual saturation of the rock.

The periglacial theory

This assumes that the chalk was frozen during the ice ages of the recent geological past and so behaved like an impermeable rock. If this was so then any summer precipitation or snowmelt would be carried away by surface streams. When the general climatic conditions became warmer the permafrosted rock would thaw and behave again as a permeable rock stratum and the water-table would fall. Thus the valleys would become dry. The Hollingbourne area, and indeed all of the North and South Downs, lay beyond the maximum limit of ice sheets, but sufficiently near it to be affected for long periods by periglacial climate conditions.

The scarp recession theory

This explanation was first advanced to explain dry valleys of the North Downs. It avoids using climatic change as a cause of a fluctuating water-table and maintains that the long-term development of the scarp and vale landscape would result in the gradual lowering of the water-table below the back-slope. As the vale is formed of weaker rocks it is eroded faster than the more resistant chalk of the escarpment. This means the scarp-foot springs are progressively lowered, and as they control the general shape of the water-table the effect will be to depress the water-table also below the back-slope, and the back-slope springs will migrate progressively down valley until the system is completely dry. Whilst this explanation appears a very logical one for the Hollingbourne dry valleys, it does involve a very long period of geological time in order to produce the very dry uplands of the present-day downs. Perhaps a combination of theories would give a more acceptable solution.

B: Ingleborough (Map 6)

This map should be studied alongside the geological map on page 63. Note that the two maps are on the same scale, 1:50,000, and cover exactly the same land area. The geology map is based on one produced in the 1:63,360 series by the Geological Survey of Britain. Concentrate first on reading the features of the topographic map; then interpretation of this map can be

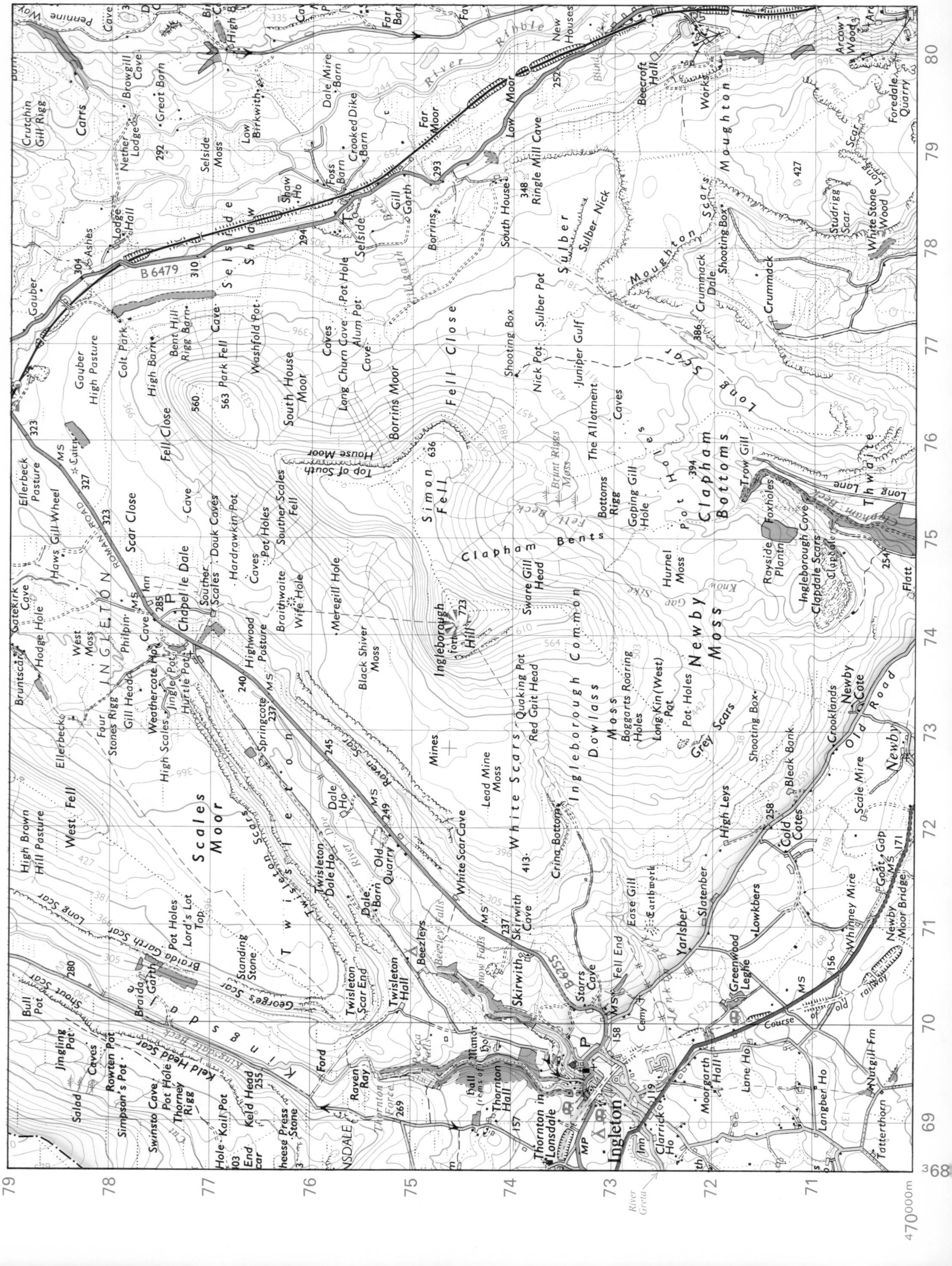
Ingleborough
Ingleton
Simon Fell
Fell Close
Park Fell
South House Moor
Borrins Moor
Top of South House Moor
Clapham Bents
Ingleborough Common
Newby Moss
Clapham Bottoms
Sulber
Moughton Scars
Moughton
Long Scar
Crummack
Crummack Dale
Selside
Selside Shaw
B 6479
B 6255
River Ribble
Gauber High Pasture
Colt Park
Scar Close
Chapel le Dale
Souther Scales Fell
Scales Moor
Twisleton Scars
Twisleton Dale Ho
White Scar Cave
White Scars
Dowlass Moss
Grey Scars
Long Churn Cave
Alum Pot
Sulber Pot
Juniper Gulf
Gaping Gill Hole
Ingleborough Cave
Clapdale Scars
Trow Gill
Hurtle Pot
Jingle Pot
Weathercote Cave
Meregill Hole
Braithwaite Wife Hole
Hardrawkin Pot
Douk Caves
Black Shiver Moss
Lead Mine Moss
Crina Bottoms
Thornton in Lonsdale
Thornton Force
Beezleys
Keld Head
Kingsdale
West Fell
Newby Cote
Newby
Cold Cotes
Old Road
470000m

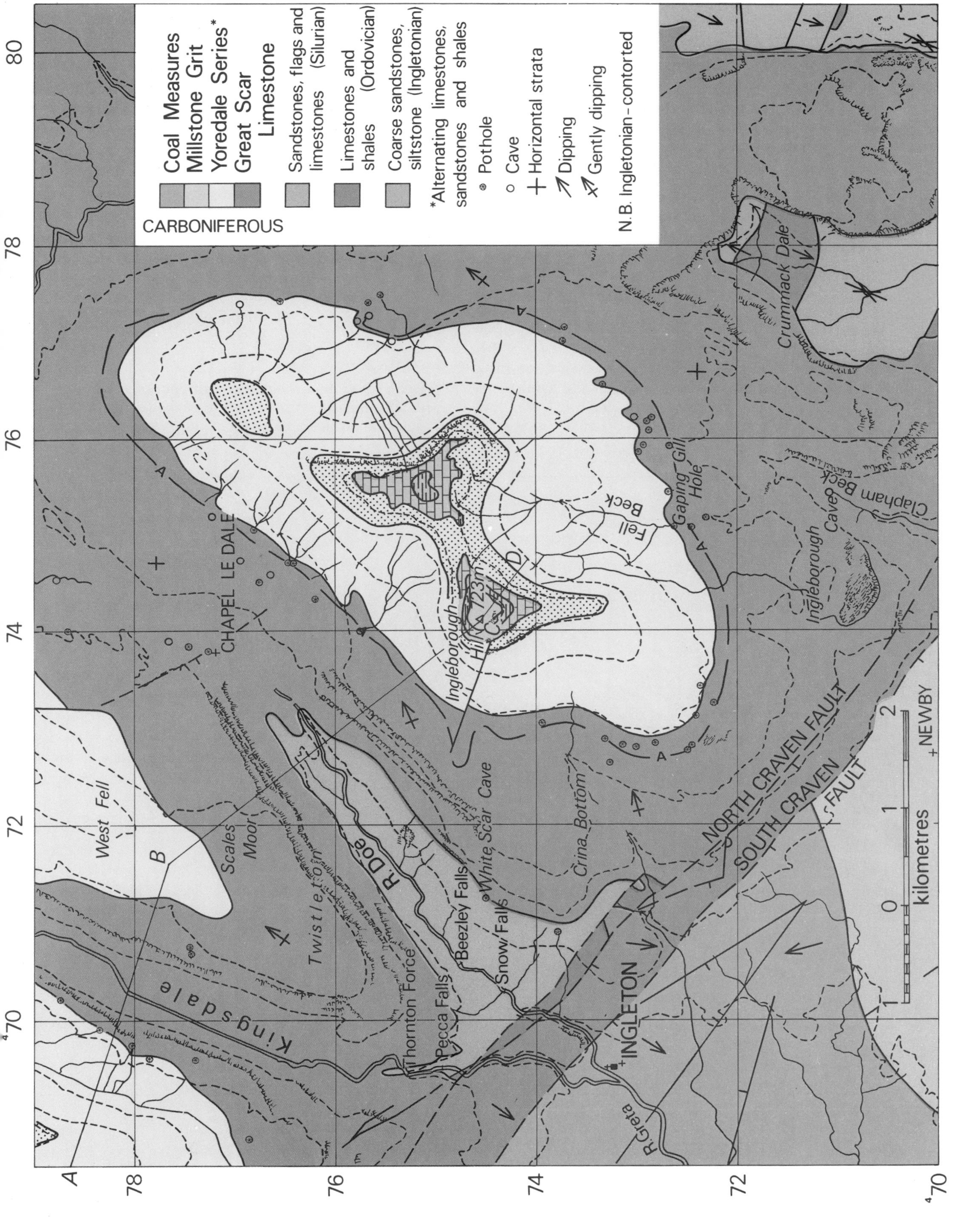
CARBONIFEROUS
Coal Measures
Millstone Grit
Yoredale Series*
Great Scar Limestone
Sandstones, flags and limestones (Silurian)
Limestones and shales (Ordovician)
Coarse sandstones, siltstone (Ingletonian)
*Alternating limestones, sandstones and shales
Pothole
Cave
Horizontal strata
Dipping
Gently dipping
N.B. Ingletonian-contorted
CHAPEL LE DALE
Ingleborough Hill
723m
Fell Beck
Gaping Gill Hole
Ingleborough Cave
Clapham Beck
Crummack Dale
West Fell
Scales Moor
Twistleton
R.Doe
White Scar Cave
Crina Bottom
Beezley Falls
Snow Falls
Thornton Force
Pecca Falls
Kingsdale
INGLETON
R.Greta
NORTH CRAVEN FAULT
SOUTH CRAVEN FAULT
NEWBY
kilometres
0
1
2
A
B
C
D
80
78
76
74
72
70

helped by examining the comparable features of the geological map. A cross-section showing relief, structure and rock outcrop along the line A–D of the geological map extract is given in Fig. 13.

This area shows a part of the Pennines in north-west Yorkshire: it is drained by three rivers—the Kingsdale Beck and river Doe which join to become the river Greta, and in the east the river Ribble. All rivers flow eventually through Lancashire to the Irish Sea. The whole area forms the district of Craven, and most of it lies within the Yorkshire Dales National Park.

Relief

This upland contrasts markedly with that shown on the previous map, Map 5 of the North Downs. The general elevation is higher and the hills are steeper with much of the surface broken into bare rock surfaces or 'scars'. But, like the limestone of the North Downs, much of this area is also very dry but there is not the same complete pattern of dry valleys; on Ingleborough and neighbouring hills the drainage pattern is broken along the valleys as streams disappear below ground.

A dissected upland block rises to 723 metres above sea-level in Ingleborough Hill. To the north-west the Kingsdale Beck and river Doe flow through steep-sided, flat-floored valleys, and to the north-east the Ribble crosses a shallower valley of more undulating relief. The major physical elements of the area are shown in the sketch-map, Fig. 38.

A platform can be seen around the hill masses at about 380 metres, e.g. on Scales Moor and all around Ingleborough. The edge of the platform is marked by the O.S. symbol for cliff-drawing, indicating broken ground, bare rock, absence of soil and vegetation cover, e.g. Twistleton Scars, Raven Scar and Keld Head Scar. The word 'scar' is a north-country term widely used in Yorkshire and Lancashire to describe steep, rocky surfaces. The lowest part of the area lies in the south-west around the small village of Ingleton.

Drainage

We can see at once the marked absence of streams in the uplands; the interrupted nature of the few that do exist suggests a surface rock of a high degree of permeability.

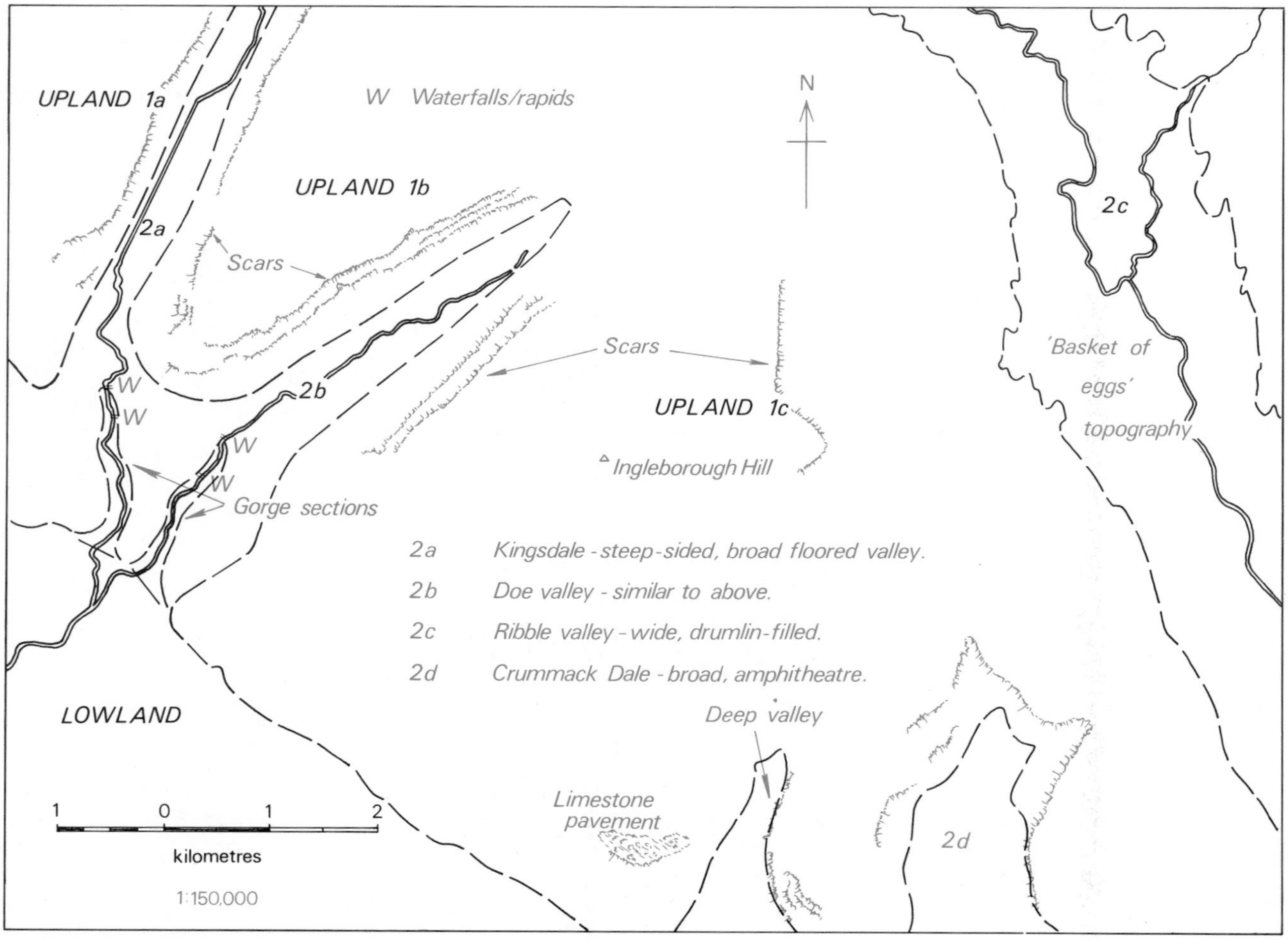

Fig. 38 Sketch-map to show physical divisions of Ingleborough map.

Closer study shows a marked spring line around the upland blocks between 250 and 300 metres with streams feeding the main rivers. On the higher slopes close to the summits there are many streams with swift but short courses. The streams peter out in pot-holes, many of which are named on the map, e.g. Meregill Hole, Gaping Gill Hole, Nick Pot. Other abandoned pot-holes are marked (e.g. 7572) which may take storm water.

The Kingsdale Beck and river Doe have gentle gradients in their upper and middle sections, but below 200 metres they suddenly flow faster in gorge sections and over waterfalls before reaching calmer waters again at Ingleton. On the other hand the Ribble flows in well-developed meanders between low hillocks, many of which are oval in plan with the long axis pointing down-valley. These small hills might prove, on field examination, to be **drumlins**, i.e. boulder clay or till deposits moulded by ice sheets.

Geology

At first sight the geology map may appear complex and confusing. The broken lines are contours selected to show the relief; they are the thickened contour lines of the topographic map. The solid lines show the geology, i.e. the various rock outcrops. Consult the key which shows the rock succession from the oldest, the Pre-Cambrian Ingletonian rocks, through the Ordovician and Silurian to the youngest geological system which covers most of the map, the Carboniferous. It should be noted that this is still a very old rock system, at least 300 million years old and part of the Primary or Palaeozoic rocks of Britain.

All the rocks are sedimentary in origin, laid down in layers as beds one above the other, but the older strata have been folded and fractured. However, the Carboniferous rocks of the area remain more or less horizontal, resting unconformably upon the older basement rocks.

The rivers and streams have cut slices through this rock sandwich so that each part of the sequence is exposed in the sides of valleys and the hills above them.

In the south-west, however, the geological structure is different; the Millstone Grit and Coal Measures forming the lowest ground have been down-thrown by the Craven faults and now butt up against the more resistant Great Scar limestone of the Ingleborough massif. The line of the South Craven fault can be traced on the 1:50,000 topographical map by the sharp break in slope following the minor road—'The Old Road'—from Ingleton to Clapham.

The many waterfalls and rapids on the streams leaving the highland block appear to be related to this major structural junction, but these features may result from other causes—e.g. changes in base level brought about by a fall in sea-level will cause rivers and streams to be rejuvenated with renewed downcutting of their valleys; the effects are first observed at the mouth of the rivers and streams and gradually progress upstream. Where the new long profile created by the renewed downcutting meets the old former profile a waterfall or rapids may be located—the so-called knickpoint. It may well be the case that rejuvenation has occurred and the knickpoints have progressed upstream until they have reached resistant rocks at the edge of the highland massif. The deep gorges cut below the falls and rapids mark the extent of their progress upstream into the resistant strata, while the wider valley profiles above the falls and rapids are the remnants of the former profiles, unaffected by the changes in base level.

The behaviour of the upland streams can also be appreciated by reference to the geology map. Examine the Ingleborough massif: the highest outcrop of the Millstone Grit series, a coarse sandstone, forms an impermeable capstone, but below this cap a limestone horizon occurs followed by a shale and these are followed in turn by the rhythmic sequence of limestones, shales and sandstones, known as the Yoredale Series. Springs emerge where permeable limestones or sandstones outcrop above impermeable shales and streams flow down the hill-sides. At the base of the Yoredale Series, marked on the map by the line –A–, the streams disappear down potholes into the Great Scar limestone, to re-emerge at the base of this limestone and join the main rivers of the area. The large number of named pot-holes and caves confirm that this is a massive limestone, strong enough to support subterranean passage-ways and caverns.

Settlement

Ingleton has developed as a foothill settlement, confluence town and route centre. Elsewhere in this area there are only hamlets in the sheltered valleys, e.g. Chapel le Dale (738772), and isolated farms at the break of slope between flood plain and valley-side. The down-faulted lower land has the highest density of habitation.

Land use

There is no indication of the nature of farming activities in the area. Presumably, in this part of Britain, the farmer will pasture sheep on the hills where rough grassland is indicated on the map, and use the wetter meadows in the valleys for cattle. There is some evidence of quarrying and mining, and present-day mineral workings are shown at 798722 and 799705. The use of the area for tourism is noticed at once by the National Park boundary, but close scrutiny reveals other signs of recreation: camping and caravan sites around Ingleton, a Youth Hostel and a viewing platform on the summit of Ingleborough Hill.

Summary

The geology map helps to confirm the interpretation of the topographic extract that this is an area of resistant rocks where the Great Scar Limestone is the main landscape former. It gives rise to typical **karst** forms where surface waters disappear down pot-holes and re-emerge through cave systems on to the impermeable and contorted Ingletonian rocks below. Similar landforms can be found in the Mendips and Peak District.

1:25 000 Second Series Map (Metric)
CONVENTIONAL SIGNS

Ordnance Survey

Roads

M I or A 6(M) Motorway

A 31 (T) Trunk road

A 35 Main road

B 3074 Secondary road

(Trunk, Main and Secondary roads:) Narrow roads with passing places are annotated

A 35 Dual carriageway

Minor road generally more than 4m tarred

Minor road generally less than 4m tarred

Minor road untarred, minor road in towns, drive or track

Unfenced roads and tracks are shown by pecked lines

Path

Public rights of way (Not applicable to Scotland)

Public paths: Footpath; Bridleway

Road used as a public path

Byway open to all traffic

Public rights of way indicated by these symbols have been derived from Definitive Maps as amended by later enactments or instruments held by Ordnance Survey on and are shown subject to the limitations imposed by the scale of mapping
The representation on this map of any other road, track or path is no evidence of the existence of a right of way

Railways

Standard gauge: Multiple track; Single track

Narrow gauge

Siding

Cutting

Embankment

Tunnel

Road over

Road under

Level crossing

Station

DANGER AREA — MOD ranges in the area
Danger! Observe warning notices

Rock Features

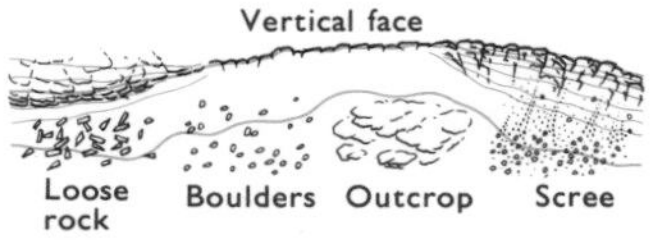

Heights

50 · ground survey
285 · air survey
(Determined by)

Surface heights are to the nearest metre above mean sea level. Heights shown close to a triangulation pillar refer to the station height at ground level and not necessarily to the summit

90, 75, 65, 60

Contours are generally at 5 metres vertical interval but on some sheets are at 10 metres VI and on others at 25 feet VI with values to the nearest metric equivalent

I metre = 3·2808 feet

Vegetation

Coniferous trees

Non coniferous trees

Coppice

Orchard

Scrub

Bracken

Heath

Rough grassland

(Bracken, Heath, Rough grassland:) Shown collectively as Rough Grassland on some sheets

Reeds

Marsh

Saltings

Symbols

Church or chapel: with tower; with spire; without tower or spire

Building

Glasshouse

Bus or coach station

Chimney

Beacon

Lighthouse

Lightship

Triangulation station

Triangulation point on church, chapel, lighthouse & beacon

Triangulation point on building & chimney

NT National Trust always open

NT National Trust opening restricted

NTS NTS National Trust for Scotland

VILLA Roman antiquity (AD 43 to AD 420)

Castle Other antiquities

Site of antiquity

1066 Site of battle (with date)

Gravel pit

Sand pit

Disused pit or quarry

Chalk pit, clay pit or quarry

Refuse or slag heap

Sloping masonry

Electricity transmission line: pylon; pole

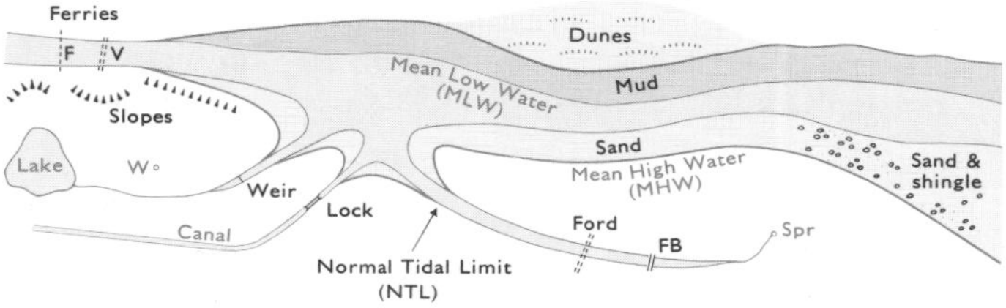

Abbreviations

BP	Boundary Post
BS	Boundary Stone
CH	Club House
F	Ferry Foot
V	Ferry Vehicle
FB	Foot Bridge
Ho	House
MP	Mile Post
MS	Mile Stone
Mon	Monument
P	Post office
Pol Sta	Police Station
PC	Public Convenience
PH	Public House
Sch	School
Spr	Spring
T	Telephone, public
A	Telephone, AA
R	Telephone, RAC
TH	Town Hall
Twr	Tower
W	Well
Wd Pp	Wind Pump
Y	Youth hostel

(P, Pol Sta, PC, PH:) Rural areas only

Boundaries

As notified to

County (England and Wales)
Region or Islands Area (Scotland)

District

London Borough

Civil Parish (England)*
Community (Wales)

Constituency (Co, Boro or Burgh)

Coincident boundaries are shown by the first appropriate symbol opposite

*For Ordnance Survey purposes County Boundary is deemed to be the limit of the parish structure whether or not a parish area adjoins

Map Border

LAT 57° 05′

01′

LAT 57° 00′

N.B. Due to changes in specification there are differences on some earlier sheets

Made and published by the Director General of the Ordnance Survey, Southampton

1:50 000 Second Series Map
CONVENTIONAL SIGNS

Ordnance Survey

ROADS AND PATHS

Not necessarily rights of way

Junction number

Service area M 1 — 3 — Elevated — Motorway (dual carriageway)

M 3 — Motorway under construction

Unfenced — Footbridge — Trunk road

A 40 (T) — Dual carriageway — Main road

Main road under construction

Secondary road

B 284 — Narrow road with passing places

A 855 — Bridge — B 885

Minor road generally more than 4m tarred

Minor road generally less than 4m tarred

Minor road untarred and minor road in towns

Path

Gradient : 1 in 5 and steeper   1 in 7 to 1 in 5

Gates   Road tunnel

Ferry P — Ferry V

Ferry (passenger)   Ferry (vehicle)

RAILWAYS

Track multiple or single

Track narrow gauge

Freight line, siding or tramway

Station (a) principal (b) closed to passengers

Level crossing (LC)

Embankment

Cutting

Bridges, Footbridge

Tunnel

Viaduct

ROCK FEATURES

PUBLIC RIGHTS OF WAY

(Not applicable to Scotland)

Footpath } Public paths

Bridleway

Road used as a public path

Byway open to all traffic

Public rights of way indicated by these symbols have been derived from Definitive Maps as amended by later enactments or instruments held by Ordnance Survey on (date) and are shown subject to the limitations imposed by the scale of mapping

The representation on this map of any other road, track or path is no evidence of the existence of a right of way.

Danger Area   MOD Ranges in the area. Danger! Observe warning notices

HEIGHTS

When standard metric contours are not available the contour interval is 50 ft with values shown to the nearest metre

50 — Contours are at 10 metres vertical interval

· 144 — Heights are to the nearest metre above mean sea level

Heights shown close to a triangulation pillar refer to the station height at ground level and not necessarily to the summit.

1 metre = 3·2808 feet   15·24 metres = 50 feet

GENERAL FEATURES

Electricity transmission line (with pylons spaced conventionally)

Radio or T V mast

Pipe line (arrow indicates direction of flow)

Church or Chapel: with tower; with spire; without tower or spire

ruin

Buildings

Public buildings (selected)

Chimney or tower

Quarry

Glasshouse

Spoil heap, refuse tip or dump

Graticule intersections at 5′ intervals

Heliport

Wood

Triangulation pillar

Orchard

Windmill with or without sails

Park or ornamental grounds

Windpump

WATER FEATURES

Marsh or salting

Lake

Canal, Lock and towpath

Canal (dry)

Aqueduct

Footbridge

Normal tidal limit

Lighthouse in use and disused

Beacon

Slopes

Cliff

Flat rock

shingle mud or sand

Low water mark

High water mark

ABBREVIATIONS

P	Post office
PH	Public house
MS ·	Milestone
M P ·	Milepost
CH	Clubhouse
PC	Public convenience (in rural areas)
TH	Town hall, Guildhall or equivalent
CG	Coastguard

ANTIQUITIES

VILLA — Roman

Castle — Non-Roman

Battlefield (with date)

Tumulus

Position of antiquity which cannot be drawn to scale

BOUNDARIES

National

London Borough

District

County, Region or Islands Area

National Park or Forest Park

NT — National Trust — always open

NT — National Trust — opening restricted

NTS (in red or blue) National Trust for Scotland

FC — Forestry Commission — Pedestrians only - observe local signs

TOURIST INFORMATION

Information Centre

Parking

Beauty spot, place of historic interest, historic house, country park, ancient monument

Picnic site

Youth hostel

Public telephone

Camp site

Golf course or links

Motoring organisation telephone

Viewpoint

Caravan site

Bus or coach station

PC — Public convenience (in rural areas)

Made and published by the Director General of the Ordnance Survey, Southampton

Chapter thirteen Glaciated highlands: The Cairngorms (Map 7 and Plate 4)

This map extract is taken from Sheet 36, Grantown and Cairngorm of the O.S. 1:50,000 Second Series. The contours are drawn at 10-metre intervals with a thickened contour line every 50 metres. Whilst this practice helps in reading the contour number it produces an impression of a 'stepped' landscape at this interval. Try to ignore this effect when estimating the form of slopes and other relief features.

At first glance the map appears bewildering and the interpretation of land forms impossible. The peaks of Cairngorm itself and Ben Macdui rise over 1,300 metres for this rugged mountain country is amongst the highest of any part of the entire British Isles, and we should expect at such altitudes to find evidence of the various glaciations that have occurred in Britain during the last two million years.

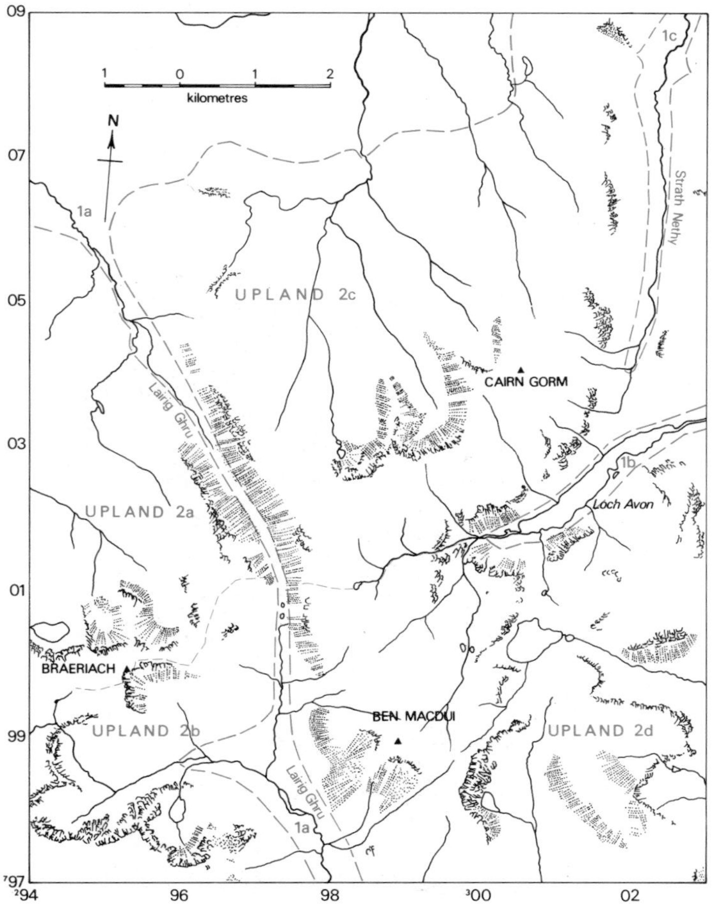

Fig. 39 Sketch-map to show physical divisions of the Cairngorm map.

To help in reading the map a glossary is given, taken from the Ordnance Survey's booklet: *Place Names on Maps of Scotland and Wales.*

Coire = corrie (cirque or cwm)	Creag = cliff, crag, rock
	Loch = lake
Beinn/ben = mountain	Lochan = small lake
Bothy = (shepherd's) hut of stone or turf	Allt = burn, stream
	Gharbh = rough
Strath = valley	Sneachda = snow

Relief

An examination of the main elements of the relief shows that a general division occurs between northern and southern parts of the map. A line taken roughly south-west and north-east and followed by the county boundary line from Braeriach (9499) separates river systems flowing northwards from those flowing east and south. But a complication to this simple division is the long through-valley or pass, the Lairig Ghru (9506 to 9897) and a more meaningful division of the map into its distinctive physical regions is shown in Fig. 39.

The valleys: Ia; Ib: Ic

The valley-sides generally are very steep indeed, especially in their lower sections, and broken rock outcrops occur frequently about the 1,000-metre contour. Scree covers the valley-sides in many places—e.g. 9898—and may reach the narrow valley floors which rise steadily to the heads of the valleys, although in Strath Nethy the northern lower part of the valley floor is flat and up to 0.25 kilometre wide. Loch Avon occupies a wide valley but its underwater profile shows an irregular floor. In the north-west the Lairig Ghru Valley leads north to the lower gentle, forested, slopes which contrast markedly with the rest of the terrain. The Lairig Ghru shows an unusual cross-profile; very steep, scree-covered slopes rise some 300 metres or more to rock faces. The actual floor is very narrow for a glacial trough while the long profile shows a low col separating the Allt Druidh from the Lairig Ghru streams, suggesting a through valley.

The mountains: IIa; IIb; IIc; IId

The highest peaks (over 1,300 metres) are Cairngorm, Ben Macdui and Braeriach, but there are many others over 1,000 metres and they all rise above steep rocky ridges which form part of characteristic armchair-shaped hollows or corries (coire), many of which contain small lakes (lochans). Around the corrie loose rock or scree is common, and the high back walls of the corrie are often extremely steep.

Drainage

As noted above, the watershed crosses the highest point of the through valley of the Lairig Ghru, and about this point there is almost a complete radial pattern of drainage. Main streams invariably flow from a corrie (whether named or not) and tumble in waterfalls to the main valleys below or into Loch Avon. Tributaries descend the sheer valley-sides with hardly a cut into the rock (see stream in 9799), i.e. with no appreciable valley channel, from the high hanging valleys.

Note that the blue 'stars' on the map are not water features but viewing points for the benefit of tourists.

Map evidence of glaciation

(a) The very large number of corries at the highest levels, many containing lakes.
(b) Behind the corries the rock walls rise to steep knife-edged ridges or arêtes.
(c) Small valleys hang above the main valley floors and waterfalls are identified by a close study of the contours, e.g. Alt a Gharb Choire—9598 and 9698, and the small valley and its river leaving grid square 0104 for the Gharb Allt.
(d) The straight courses of many streams hardly incised into the valley sides suggests that they are of Recent, i.e. postglacial origin—see streams draining into Loch Avon.
(e) Loch Avon appears to lie in a natural over-deepened rock basin.
(f) Although there are no valleys with the typical flat floor of the U-shaped glaciated valley, the sides are straight, very steep, and former spurs truncated—see Lairig Ghru and Strath Nethy. Some of these features are shown in Fig. 39. Compare also with Figs. 21a and 21b.

Settlement

This is a wild and desolate place. With the exception of Rothiemurchus Lodge (952069) there is no sign of permanent habitation. The only buildings are mountain huts and refuges for those exploring the area or sheltering from severe weather conditions. The perilous nature of this area is reflected in a number of memorial mountain shelters.

Communications

There is no railway and no major roads of any kind; a minor road capable of carrying motorised transport leads through the northern forest to the foot of the ski-lift. Otherwise there are only ride-ways through the forest and innumerable footpaths following not only the easier route-ways along the valleys but also crossing the mountains from peak to peak.

Land use

Man can make only a very limited use of terrain of this kind. The land is too high, too steep and rugged and too exposed for any sort of cultivation. Sheep-raising is a possibility, but there is little evidence of it on the map save for the Bothy, 9598 (now a mountain hut) and White Lady Shieling, 9905 (a sheepfold). The north-western area is forested where slopes are more gentle and the land is lower and the map shows the southern edge of a National or Forest Park. The principal use of this land today is clearly for recreational purposes. Apart from the climbing huts there are four special viewing sites and a number of ski-tows and a chair-lift in grid square 9905.

Although the rock is evidently hard and resistant to erosion there is nothing on the map to suggest quarrying or mining in any way.

Summary

The abundant water indicates an impermeable bedrock, but there is no named evidence of rock type. The evidence of highland glaciation is overwhelming and indicates collection of snow and ice during the Ice Age and the outward movement of glaciers to lower elevations. Associated with this intensive glaciation was the cutting of the deep Lairig Ghru Pass—whether entirely by ice is not clear from map evidence alone—but it resulted in the breaching of a former east-west main watershed.

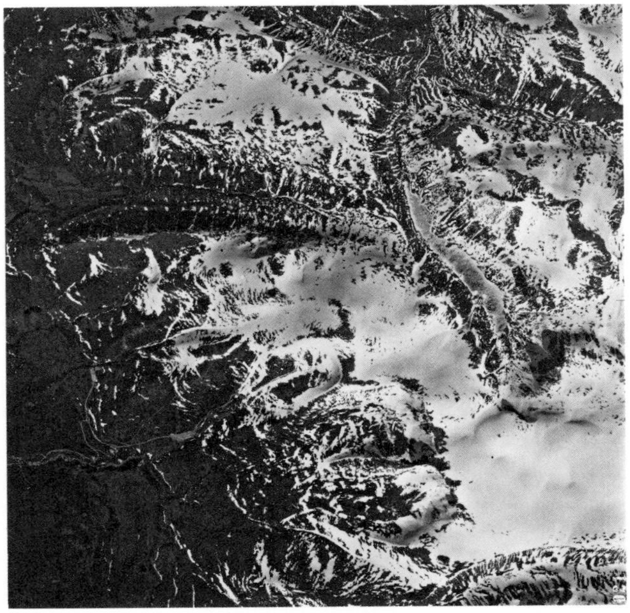

PLATE 4 Loch Avon and Cairngorm

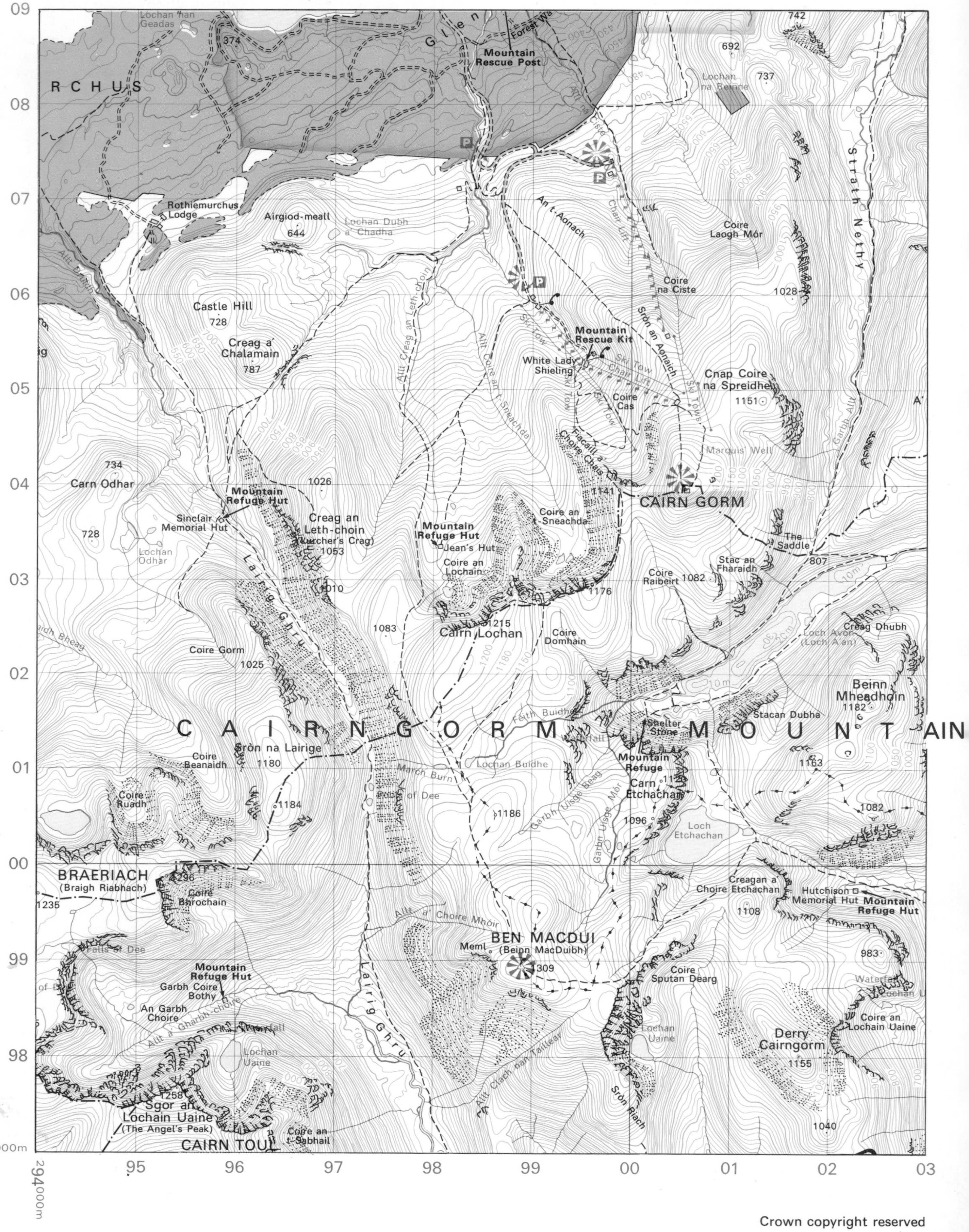
Lochan nan Geadas
Glen
Forest Way
Mountain Rescue Post
RCHUS
Lochan na Beinne
692
737
742
Strath Nethy
Rothiemurchus Lodge
Airgiod-meall
644
Lochan Dubh a' Chadha
An t-Aonach
Chair Lift
Coire Laogh Mór
Coire na Ciste
1028
Castle Hill
728
Creag a' Chalamain
787
Mountain Rescue Kit
White Lady Shieling
Ski Tow
Sròn an Aonaich
Cnap Coire na Spreidhe
1151
Coire Cas
Marquis' Well
Fiacaill a' Choire Chais
1141
CAIRN GORM
Allt Creag an Leth-choin
Allt Coire an t-Sneachda
734
Carn Odhar
728
Mountain Refuge Hut
Sinclair Memorial Hut
Lochan Odhar
1026
Creag an Leth-choin
(Lurcher's Crag)
1053
Mountain Refuge Hut
Jean's Hut
Coire an t-Sneachda
Coire an Lochain
1176
The Saddle
807
Stac an Fharaidh
Coire Raibeirt
1082
Lairig Ghru
1010
1083
1215
Cairn Lochan
Coire Domhain
Creag Dhubh
Loch Avon
(Loch A'an)
Coire Gorm
1025
Beinn Mheadhoin
1182
Stacan Dubha
CAIRNGORM MOUNTAIN
Feith Buidhe
Shelter Stone
Sròn na Lairige
1180
Coire Beanaidh
Mountain Refuge
Carn Etchachan
1163
Lochan Buidhe
March Burn
Pools of Dee
Coire Ruadh
1184
1186
Garbh Uisge Beag
Garbh Uisge Mór
1096
Loch Etchachan
1082
BRAERIACH
(Braigh Riabhach)
1296
Coire Bhrochain
1235
Creagan a' Choire Etchachan
1108
Hutchison Memorial Hut
Mountain Refuge Hut
Allt a' Choire Mhóir
BEN MACDUI
(Beinn MacDuibh)
Meml.
1309
Falls of Dee
Mountain Refuge Hut
Garbh Coire Bothy
983
Coire Sputan Dearg
An Garbh Choire
Allt a' Gharbh-choire
Lochan Uaine
Lochan Uaine
Coire an Lochain Uaine
Derry Cairngorm
1155
Allt Clach nan Taillear
Sròn Riach
1258
Sgor an Lochain Uaine
(The Angel's Peak)
CAIRN TOUL
Coire an t-Sabhail
1040
797000m
294000m
95
96
97
98
99
00
01
02
03

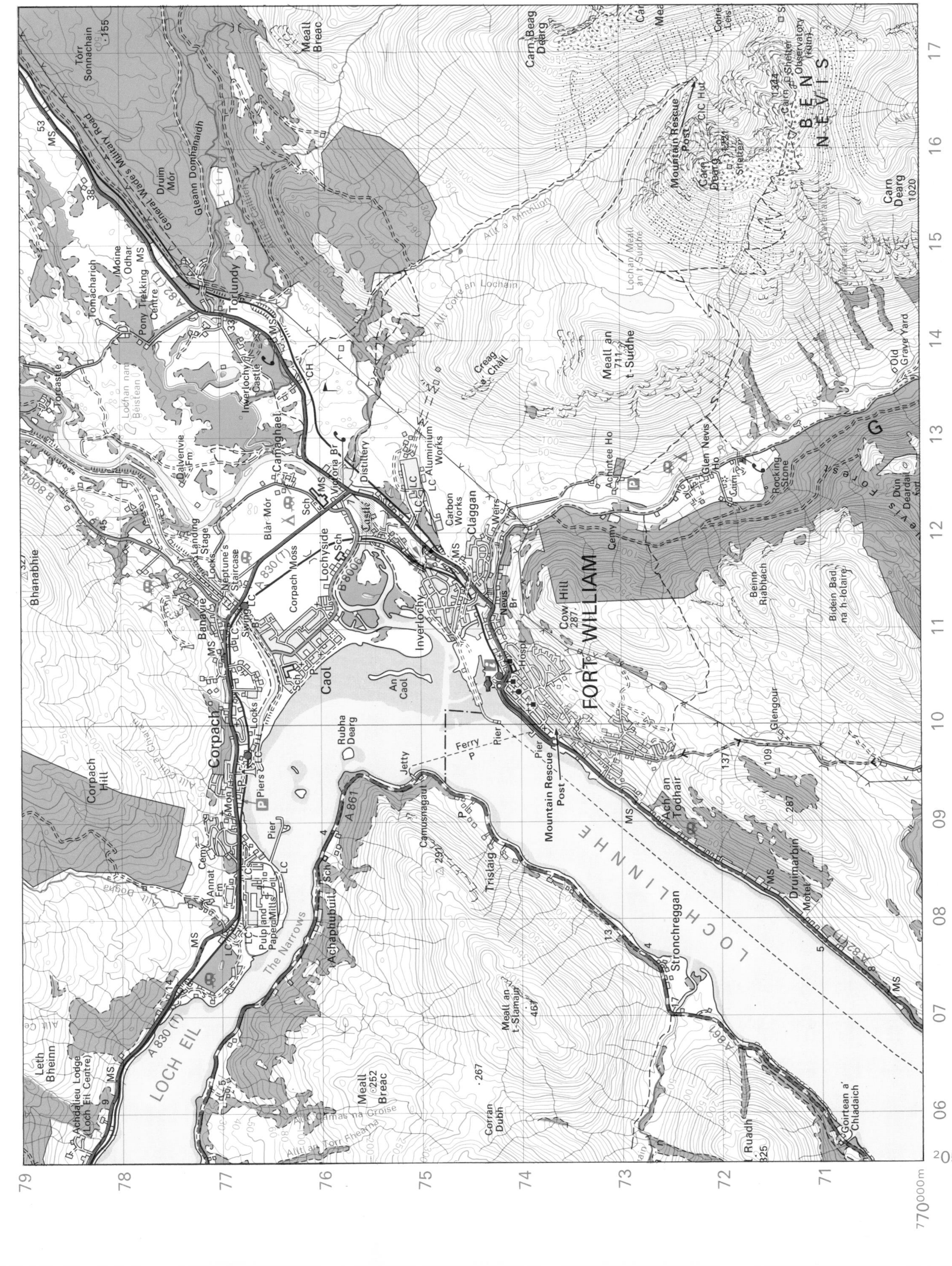
FORT WILLIAM
LOCH LINNHE
LOCH EIL
BEN NEVIS
Corpach
Corpach Hill
Caol
An Caol
Banavie
Bhanabhie
Inverlochy
Inverlochy Castle
Lochyside
Camaghael
Torlundy
Claggan
Blàr Mòr
Corpach Moss
Neptune's Staircase
Landing Stage
Cow Hill 287
Meall an t-Suidhe 711
Carn Dearg 1020
Carn Beag Dearg
Meall Breac
Druim Mòr
Gleann Domhanaidh
Tòrr Sonnachain
Moine Odhar
Tomacharich
Pony Trekking Centre
Torcastle
Dalvenie Fm
Lochan nam Beistean
General Wade's Military Road
Aluminium Works
Carbon Works
Distillery
Victoria Br
Nevis Br
Glen Nevis Ho
Achintee Ho
Rocking Stone
Dùn Deardail
Old Grave Yard
Beinn Riabhach
Bidein Bad na h-Iolaire
Glengour
Ach an Todhair
Druimarbin
Motel
Mountain Rescue Post
CIC Hut
Observatory (Ruin)
Camusnagaul
Trislaig
Stronchreggan
Meall an t-Slamain 467
Meall Breac 252
Corran Dubh
Achaphubuil
The Narrows
Pulp and Paper Mills
Annat Fm
Achdalieu Lodge (Loch Eil Centre)
Leth Bheinn
Goirtean a' Chladaich
Rubha Dearg
Ferry
Pier
Jetty
A 830 (T)
A 82 (T)
A 861
B 8004
B 8006
770000m
205500m

Chapter fourteen Settlement, communications and industry:
A: Fort William (Map 8 and Plate 5)
B: Alloa (Map 9 and Plate 1)

A: Fort William (Map 8 and Plate 5)

Settlement, communications and industry are strongly controlled in this area by its physical geography. Settlement is dominated by Fort William and its satellite settlement, Corpach. All signs of habitation are confined to the loch side, the Lochy Valley and Glen Nevis; hardly a single building can be found on the higher ground.

Communications

The earliest exploration of the area was probably by water, the explorers coming along the western coast of Scotland and travelling up the long sea inlets (see photo, Plate 5). Water communication is still important but supplemented by well-established roads and rail route-ways. None the less most of the interior can only be reached on foot.

Water communication

The broken line along Loch Linnhe shows the deep-water course followed by boats from the open sea making for Fort William pier. Note how the pier, and that near Corpach, extend beyond the mudbanks into deeper water (cf. Plate 5). A shorter ferry crossing to Camusnagaul leaves from a smaller pier by the main road. Piers are also seen at the entrance to the Caledonian Canal to provide mooring for the small craft using the canal which have some difficulty negotiating the gradient at the margin of the valley. The numerous lochs required in this operation are aptly named Neptune's Staircase (114770).

Road communication

The main road, A82(T) runs north-east to Inverness. It occupies the whole of the lake shore along Loch Linnhe as far as Fort William, and then keeps to the eastern edge of the Lochy flood plain. In the north-east of the area the modern road runs parallel to General Wade's Military Road, one of many such Highland roads built for the English armies after the Jacobite rebellions.

A second major road, A830(T) crosses the lower flood plain of the Lochy, turns west through Corpach and keeps close to the northern shore of Loch Eil. On the opposite shore the A861 is even more restricted by relief as the map symbol is that for a narrow road with passing places.

Rail communication

Considering the difficulties of road construction it is not surprising to find the railway exploiting the same limited flat land and generally running parallel to the two trunk roads. This line connects the western ferry port of Mallaig with Fort William and Glasgow. Note that it crosses the Caledonian Canal by means of a swing bridge.

Industry

Plate 5 shows several large buildings that could be factories located on the alluvial land close to the pier and to the railway. The map shows in plan and actually names other industrial sites: these are shown in Fig. 40. Near the Victoria Bridge (124757) conveniently situated to take water from the Allt a' Mhuilinn is a Distillery, presumably for whisky (B on sketch-map). Just south of the Distillery can be found an industrial complex comprising an Aluminium Works and a Carbon Works (C and D on sketch-map). The advantages of this site judged from the map evidence are:

(i) flat land for building large works;
(ii) proximity to railway for sidings and carriage of bulky freight;
(iii) proximity to main road for other supplies and for personnel;
(iv) proximity to pierhead for importing raw materials and despatching aluminium products;
(v) availability of hydro-electricity from adjacent upland (note the pipe-line symbol), and other power from main transmission line.

The Pulp and Paper Mills at Corpach (A on sketch-map) have very similar advantages of site and situation utilising the flatter land around the mouth of a small river, the Allt Dogha.

Other activities named or shown by map symbols relate to the very important tourist industry in this area. This can be seen in the provision of camping and caravan sites, climbing huts, picnic sites, a pony-trekking centre, hotels and hostels. For all these activities Fort William is the centre and here is marked the symbol for Tourist Information Centre.

PLATE 5 Fort William

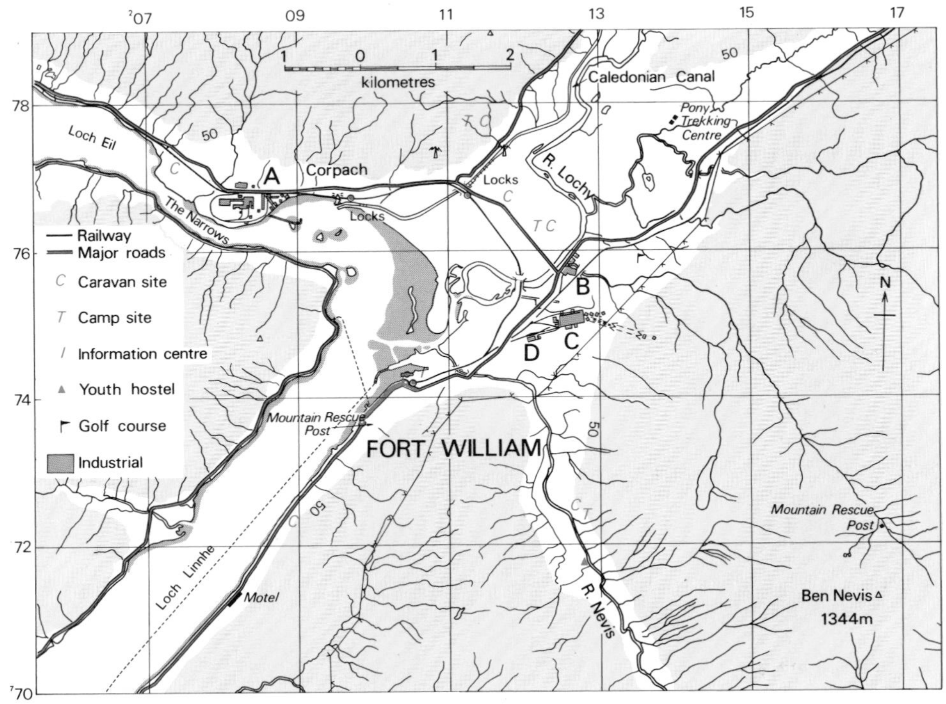

Fig. 40 Sketch-map of communications and industries of the Fort William map.

B: Alloa (Map 9 and Plate 1)

We can now turn from the analysis of relief and drainage and concentrate on settlement. This map extract of part of the East Central Lowlands includes in the north part of the Ochil Hills, one of a chain of igneous rock uplands forming the Northern Heights in the Midland Rift Valley of Scotland. It is clear that there has been a strong control by land and water features over the pattern of settlement and communications.

Settlement

There are no large towns to be seen on the map but many small nucleated settlements do appear. These include Alloa, a line of foothill towns, Alva, Tillicoultry and Dollar, and a few other scattered dwellings.

The site

This covers approximately 5 square kilometres between low hills and the river Forth; it is everywhere below the 30 metre contour line and is confined entirely to the north bank. The site takes advantage of a relatively deep water frontage (absence of mud shoals and sandbanks) at a point where the river begins to widen into the estuary.

The situation

The river is very important to the town. Upstream to the north-west navigation would be difficult because of the numerous mudbanks, sandbanks and islands. Bridge building appears to have been impossible until the railway era and it is noteworthy that Alloa Bridge selects a narrow channel between a peninsula of firm ground to the north, and a gravel bank to the south. A crossing-point from south Alloa to the main town would probably have hindered navigation and imposed considerable engineering difficulties.

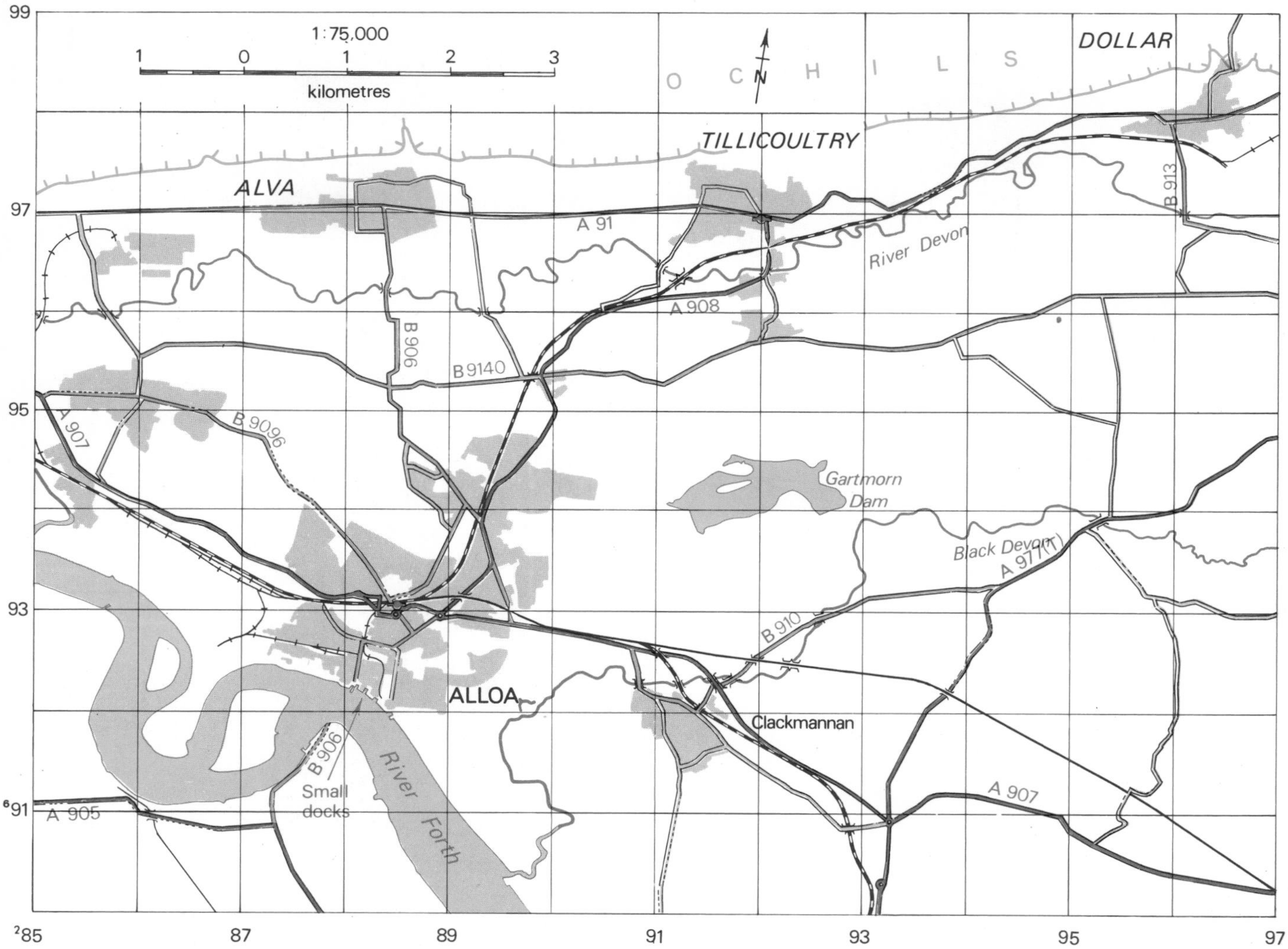

Fig. 41 Sketch-map of communications on map of Alloa.

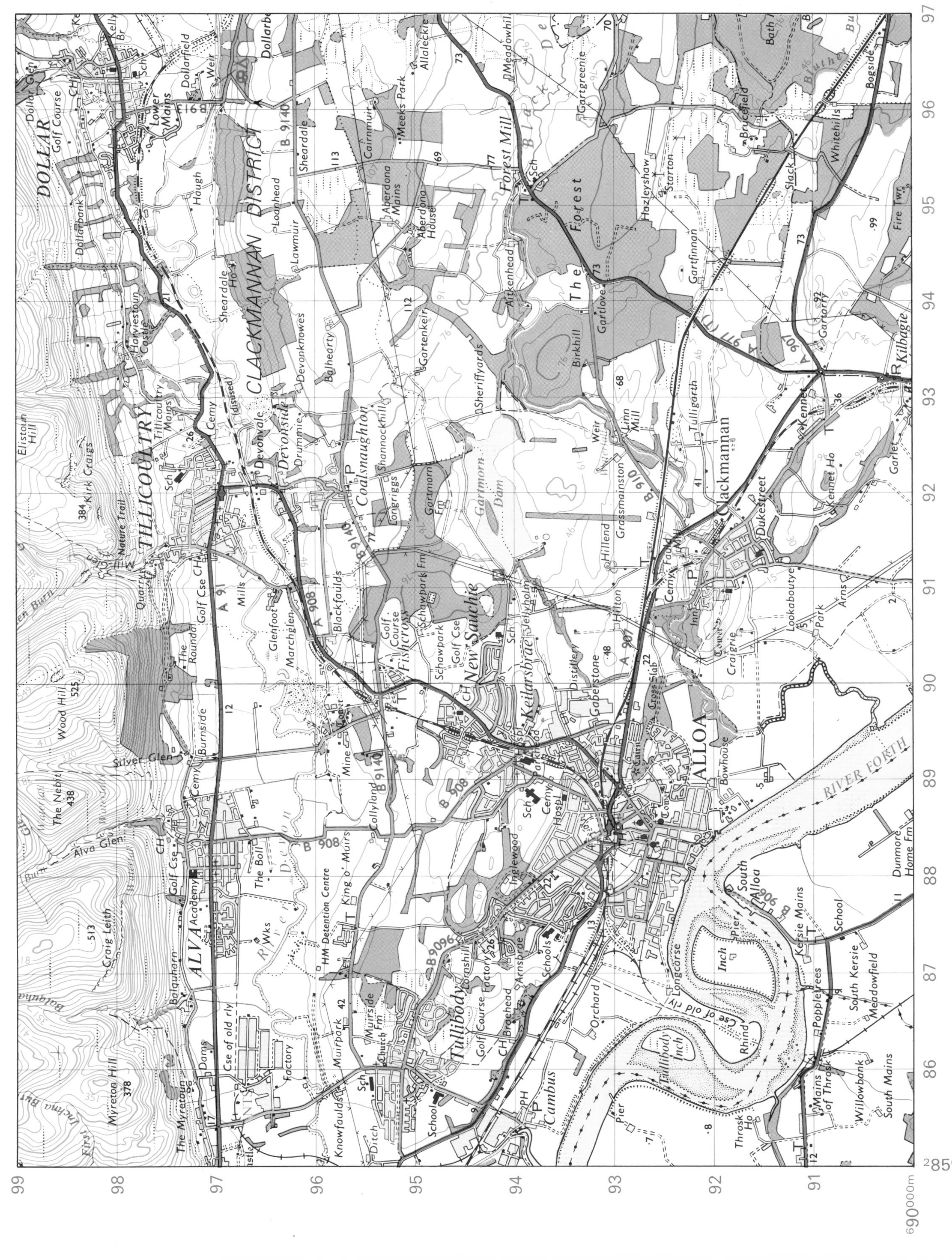
ALLOA
ALVA
TILLICOULTRY
DOLLAR
CLACKMANNAN DISTRICT
Clackmannan
Tullibody
Cambus
New Sauchie
Coalsnaughton
Devonside
Fishcross
The Forest
Forest Mill
Kennet
Kilbagie
RIVER FORTH
Tullibody Inch
South Alloa
Gartmorn Dam
Keilarsbrae
Dollarbank
Harviestoun Castle
HM Detention Centre
Cse of old rly
285000m
690000m

Function

In spite of the absence of a road bridge the network of communication indicates the importance of the town, with its symbols showing both a main-line railway station and a bus and coach terminal. Port facilities include piers, open river docks, and a dock basin which are served by a dock railway. The evidence of industry is lacking, only the name 'Distillery' indicating an occupation.

The foothill towns

All are located on similar sites, and have the same situation with regard to relief.

The site

It is remarkable how the small towns of Tillicoultry and Alva have sought out a narrow platform of raised ground encompassed by the 15-metre contour, lying well away from the river and flanked by steeply rising ground to the north. The factors that are probably responsible for the development of the site of Alva can be seen in Fig. 27. The map shows that Tillicoultry has grown on a similar site and a study of Dollar reveals that although the general height is around 30 metres, the site characteristics are essentially the same as the other two towns.

The situation

All three towns lie in the corridor of lowland in the valley of the river Devon on the northern margin of its flood plain between the low undulating hills in the middle of the map and the barrier of highlands to the north. Of minor importance, perhaps, in the situation of the three towns is the protection given by the highlands from northerly gales, and the southerly aspect which favours sunshine and warmth.

Functions

These towns are too small to support much industry and the map evidence for it is scanty. A large factory at Menstrie, 858965, is served by a railway, although the village is very small and the station closed to passengers. This suggests that Menstrie is a suburb of a larger town, or that workers are brought by road from some distance. Mill Glen, occupied by a fast-moving stream above Tillicoultry, may indicate an old industrial site and this town is the terminus of the main line section of the railway from Alloa, suggesting a place of some importance at the present time or at least in the recent past.

The other settlements on the map are scattered, and for the most part no more than small villages. Only Clackmannan and Tullibody deserve our attention. Clackmannan is a small nucleated settlement to the south of the Black Devon river, on the sides of a small knoll overlooking the Forth Valley. A main road passes through the town but the village is served only by a single-track railway and the station is closed. At Tullibody the form of the built-up area as shown by map symbols suggests a relatively modern development and this is confirmed somewhat by the absence of an old central nucleus and parish church. The railway bypasses the settlement well to the south.

Communications

We can appreciate best the pattern of communications by preparing a reduced sketch-map. Figure 41 shows clearly the strong control over the road and rail network exercised by the physical features. The highlands in the north prevent access by road and rail; only footpaths are shown in this northern area on the O.S. map. The uplands between the Devon and Forth valleys are nowhere high enough to prevent construction of roads and the railways can easily overcome the low gradients by means of short cuttings. As for the influence of the main water channel, that of the Forth, reference has been made above to the problem of bridge construction and the navigational hazards of the river channel.

Summary

From his knowledge of the regional geography of Scotland the student should recognise in the name Clackmannan once one of Scotland's five major coalfields, but on this map only one mine is marked, at Fishcross, 898958.

We have some reasons from the map for the settlement and communication layout of this part of the Scottish lowlands. The obvious physical control of the foothill towns and the limitation on the growth of Alloa imposed by the Forth river and its valley can be deduced from the map, but there is a marked lack of information relating to occupations.

Chapter fifteen Urban land use: Warwick and Leamington (Map 10 and Plate 6)

The two maps, Figs. 42a and 42b show the use of land in the twin boroughs of Warwick and Leamington in the English Midlands. The differences between the two maps demonstrate the difficulties of map interpretation: Fig. 42a shows a careful interpretation of all the map evidence provided by the O.S. 1:25,000 topographic map extract (Map 10), whilst Fig. 42b shows how further information, obtained 'in the field' can verify the first interpretation, correct it and extend it. The supplementary information on Fig. 42b was obtained on the ground by walking and driving through the two settlements and by consulting maps in the County Planning Department and Public Record Office in Warwick. Note that the maps have been reduced slightly from the original 1:25,000 scale.

Map 10 shows two urban sites, densely settled but separated by the shallow valley of the river Avon and its tributary, the Leam. The Avon appears to have served effectively as a southern boundary to the growth of Warwick except for the satellite settlement at Bridge End where the present Castle Bridge brings traffic across the river. Otherwise the building line stops at the northern and western edge of the flood plain, or at the river cliff which rises to over 60 metres (see Plate 6). Above the cliff was built Warwick Castle and below it at the Weir there are the remains of an ancient bridge, presumably the first crossing place. At some later time the bridging point carrying the road leading to the town centre was moved downstream to its present position, the route skirting the eastern end of the castle.

Main roads follow higher ground and, even today, avoid the flood plains of the valley floor. The northern section of the Avon valley still consists of open land separating the two towns, and significantly the official boundary between the boroughs runs along the middle of the river. Apart from the bridge-crossings which forge north-south linkages across the Avon and Leam valleys the most important routes run south-west to north-east, that one through Warwick being, quite literally, the 'High Street' (Plate 6). Other factors clearly influencing the settlement pattern are the canal and the railway lines. Industrial 'Works' and housing estates have been built alongside these communication spines, dating presumably from the late eighteenth and early nineteenth centuries which were the great periods of canal and railway building.

Thus it is possible, as shown in Fig. 42a, to recognise certain topographic evidence and prepare, on this basis alone, a map of land use. Proceed as follows:

1. Identify Warwick Castle and the remains of the bridge. These are named in an ancient script and, therefore, can be considered medieval in age.
2. The 'old core' of Warwick can be inferred from high density of generally unplanned buildings in the town centre. Within the core there are many churches indicating small parishes (formerly well-populated). The limit of the core is not always easy to see and the boundary ill-defined.

   There is no such obvious 'core' in Leamington, but in the town centre—and also to the north-east of the central districts of Warwick—can be found a marked rectilinear pattern of streets and terraced housing suggesting building development of the eighteenth and nineteenth centuries in Georgian and early Victorian England (see 'X' on Fig. 42a).
3. Moving outside these areas and to the outskirts of the two towns a more open pattern of estate building can be discovered. Wide main roads lead to crescents and cul-de-sacs where are found small terraces and semi-detached properties with rear gardens, all very reminiscent of building in the inter- and post-war periods. Note particularly the housing estates at Whitnash (3263) and Milverton (3066)—'C' on Fig. 42a.
4. Industrial buildings may be identified in a number of places, sometimes by the size and shape of the buildings or by their location close to the railway line or canal, or by named evidence of 'Works'. It is not, however, possible to determine the nature of the industrial activity although there are obvious differences in the scale of operations, e.g. contrast the large industrial site marked 'A' on Fig. 42a with the small works along the canal banks in grid square 2965—marked 'B'.
5. Other specialised land use that can be mapped includes schools, colleges, the racecourses, sewage works, hospitals and other public buildings.

Now turn to Fig. 42b and compare the mapped data derived from town surveys and by fieldwork. Much more detail can be shown both of function and of periods of growth. It can now be seen that 'A' of Fig. 42a is an industrial complex of works built at different times, and that there are many more industrial units than those deduced from map evidence alone. It has also been possible to add to the map new buildings which were not there when the O.S. last revised the 1:25,000 map in 1974, and to show conservation areas.

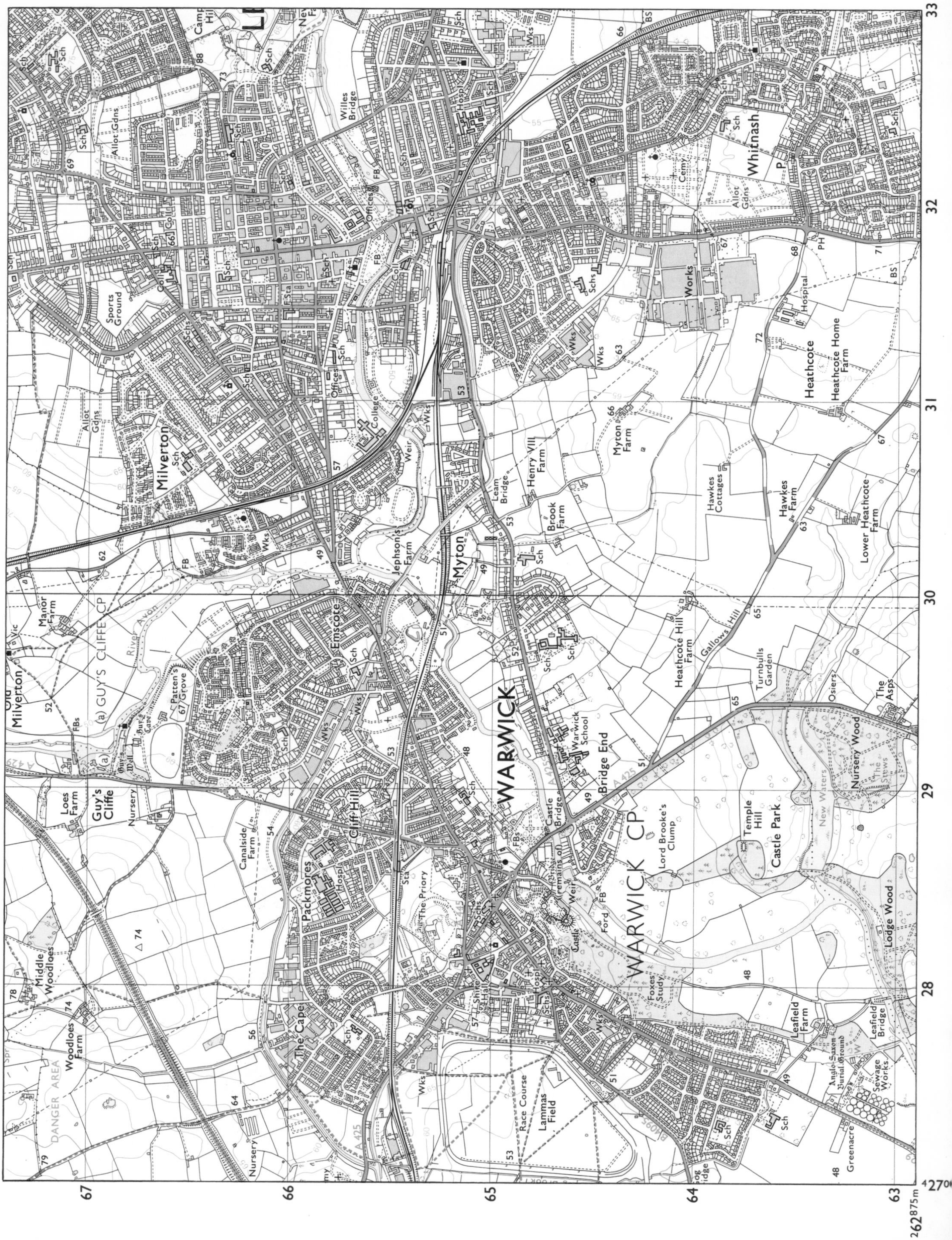
WARWICK
Whitnash
Milverton
Old Milverton
Emscote
Myton
Heathcote
WARWICK CP
(a) GUY'S CLIFFE CP
Guy's Cliffe
Castle Park
Packmores
Cliff Hill
The Cape
Race Course
Lammas Field
Bridge End
Warwick School
Lodge Wood
Nursery Wood
Temple Hill
Lord Brooke's Clump
Manor Farm
Woodloes Farm
Middle Woodloes
Loes Farm
Canalside Farm
Jephson's Farm
Henry VIII Farm
Brook Farm
Myton Farm
Hawkes Cottages
Hawkes Farm
Lower Heathcote Farm
Heathcote Home Farm
Heathcote Hill Farm
Gallows Hill
Turnbulls Garden
The Asps
Osiers
New Waters
The Stews
Leafield Farm
Leafield Bridge
Sewage Works
Anglo-Saxon Burial Ground
Greenacre
Foxes Study
Sports Ground
DANGER AREA
The Priory
Castle Bridge
Lean Bridge
Willes Bridge
Patten's Grove
River Avon
Works
Hospital
Nursery
67
66
65
64
63
33
32
31
30
29
28
4270
262875m

Fig. 42a Urban land use, by map interpretation – Warwick and Leamington.

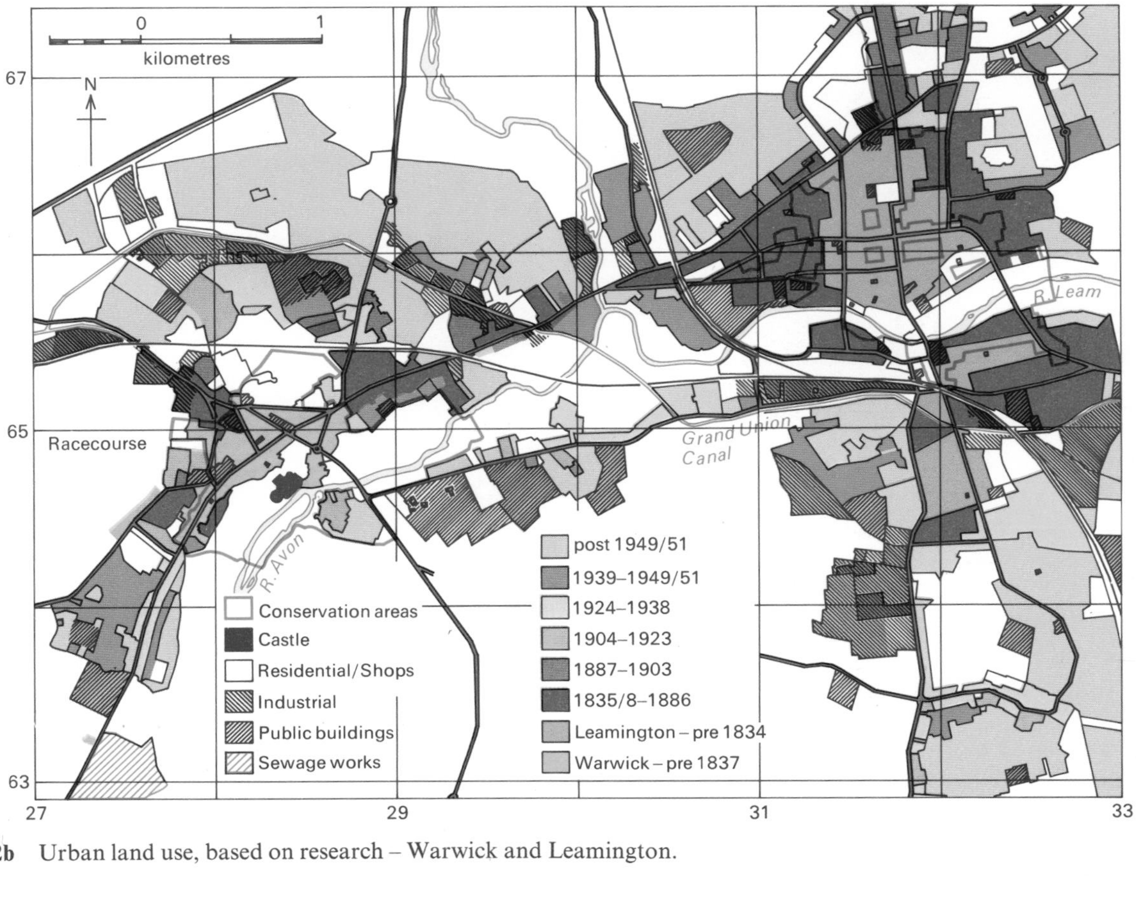

Fig. 42b Urban land use, based on research – Warwick and Leamington.